JECT M

CAN SUBJ

MATTER CA

BJECT M

MATTER

MATTER CA

ITBYBIT

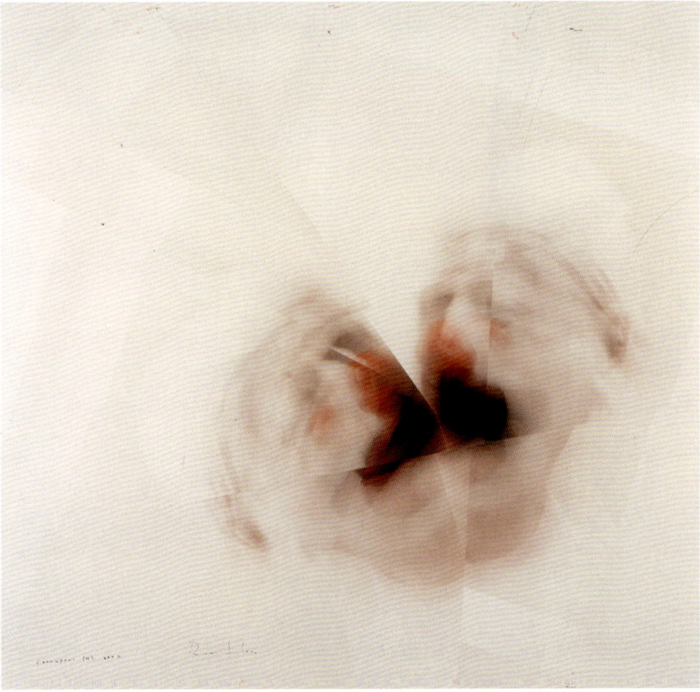

IT BY BIT

Prescott Muir
Introduction by Juhani Pallasmaa
Foreword by Dan Hoffman

ORO

In memory of Jim Pulliam, who paid it elegantly forward,
and to Sharon for her continuing steadfast support.

TABLE OF CONTENTS

ON ARCHITECTURAL SYNTAX AND ATMOSPHERE

by Juhani Uolevi Pallasmaa

BOTH IN HIS WORDS and designs, Prescott Muir is engaged in processes of emergent architectural meanings arising from the interaction of distinct architectural principles, intellectual assumptions, precedents and conventions, as well as deliberate personal innovations.[1] Although not basing his work on the theories of Deconstructivism, Muir seems to keep dismantling or deconstructing the architectural, syntax, and then recomposing it for each one of his projects.

Muir is interested in the dialectics of predictability and unpredictability, the deterministic and autonomous ingredients in architectural design. "Could there be an element of predictability in design where you concede authorship and the trappings of ego in favour of some autonomous and indeed anonymous system ...?" he asks.[2]

Reading Muir's thoughts on architecture and looking at images of his projects and executed work, invited me to ponder on the essence of mental structures in architecture, as well as their experiential impacts.

DISMANTLING THE ARCHITECTURAL IMAGE

Every architectural project is suspended between the silent traditions of the discipline and the desire for novelty and individual expression. Every profound piece of architecture is simultaneously about the world, the specificities of the task, and the internal essence of architecture. This silent dialogue implies the dismantling and re-fusion of the architectural syntax: a study of the relations of the whole and the parts, the autonomous and the interfused, and the roles of recalling and re-creating. An understanding of the dialectics of image and experience, recognition and affect, deduction and emotion, evocation and affect, is also called for.

What is the structure of architectural experience, and what are the mechanics of architectural meaning? What is the true focus of architectural intention, and which are the means for the materialization of these intentions and meanings? What are the true goals and means, objectives and steps, in the process of architectural design?

Since Vitruvius Pollio's *Ten Books of Architecture,* architecture has been analyzed and theorized for more than two millennia, but it seems that the ways in which a profound and moving architectural entity is created continue to be rather vaguely understood. What is its real inner structure, as well as the experiential and mental cohesion of the image that draws us into its spell and keeps feeding our imagination?

The established theoretical views of the art form of architecture seem applicable for a purely formal approach, but hardly meaningful for the experiential and mental essences and impacts of architecture. The field of architectural experience is lived and existential rather than formal.

The dominant linguistic theories continue to place human meaning in words and structures of language, and the origin of the language is seen in the emergence of the word. However, convincing linguistic studies have established the role of the mental image, or neural pattern, as the basis of all linguistic realities, or for that matter, any recognition, cognition, or remembrance. Shouldn't architecture, also, look for the hidden mental realities of buildings and acts of construction rather than the overt formal material and conventions?

One of the problems in understanding the mental essence of architecture seems to arise from the received tendency of Western thought to explain phenomena from their constitutive elements upwards towards the whole. Yet, the innate singularity of a true artistic or architectural entity obtains its coherence and meaning from the entity down towards its ingredients, elements, and details. Indeed, an isolated idea, suggestion or detail in any work of art is meaningless without the entity that provides the ground and syntax of meaning; an isolated detail may well be technically and aesthetically interesting, but in its isolation it is bound to remain without meaning, as it arises from the integrating mental image of the work.

IN PRAISE OF ATMOSPHERE

One of the least understood and theorized aspects of architectural effect is its atmosphere, or ambience. The atmosphere of a poem, painting, or piece of architecture is the overarching and integrating perceptual, sensory and emotive impression, the "experiential and emotive structure" of the work, as it were.

The character of a space or place is not merely a visual quality as is usually assumed. This judgment of environmental character is a complex fusion of countless factors which are immediately and synthetically grasped as an overall atmosphere, mood or ambience. "I enter a building, see a room, and—in the fraction of a second—have this feeling about it," Peter Zumthor confesses.[3] This experience is multisensory in its very essence, but it also involves judgments beyond the five received Aristotle an senses. This multidimensional and simultaneous perception calls for such capacities as the senses of orientation, gravity, balance, stability, motion, duration, continuity and scale. Indeed, the immediate judgement of the character of space calls for our entire embodied and existential sense, and it is perceived in a diffuse and peripheral manner rather than through precise and conscious observation. We sense through our entire embodied constitutions rather than through any singular sense. Moreover, this complex judgment fuses perception, memory and imagination. Even perceptions and recollections are actively created, and are not products of automatic or mindless sensory mechanisms.

In addition to environmental atmosphere, there are cultural, social, workplace, etc. atmospheres which play a significant role in our behaviour and personal moods. Of the various art forms, music is particularly atmospheric, and has a forceful impact on our emotions and moods regardless of how little or how much we intellectually understand musical structures. The same instantaneous and involuntary character applies to the impact of natural and architectural settings.

Sir Colin St. John Wilson explains this irresistible force:

> It is as if I am being manipulated by some subliminal code, not to be translated into words, which acts directly on the nervous system and imagination, at the same time stirring intimations of meaning with vivid spatial experience as though they were one thing. It is my belief that the code acts so directly and vividly upon us because it is strangely familiar; it is in fact the first language we ever learned, long before words, and which is now recalled to us through art, which alone holds the key to revive it ....[4]

As we enter a space, the space enters us, and the experience is essentially an exchange and fusion. Robert Pogue Harrison, the American literary scholar, states poetically: "In the fusion of place and soul, the soul is as much of a container of place as place is a container of soul; both are susceptible to the same forces of destruction."[5]

Paradoxically, we grasp the atmosphere of a place before we identify details or understand it intellectually. In fact, we may be completely unable to say anything meaningful about the characteristics of a place, yet have a firm image, emotive attitude, and recall of it. As we enter a new city, we grasp its character similarly, without having consciously analyzed a single one of its myriad properties. This is an intuitive and emotive capacity that seems to be biologically derived and largely unconsciously and instinctively determined through evolutionary programming. "We perceive atmospheres through our emotional sensibility—a form of perception that works incredibly quickly, and which we humans evidently need to help us survive," Peter Zumthor assumes.[6]

A space or a place is an image, a mental or neural "creature," an experiential singularity that is fused with our very existential experience and cognition. We can remember a complex entity, such as a landscape, through its integrating image, its ambience, rather than as an assembly of visual parts. Once we have assessed a space as inviting and pleasant, or uninviting and depressing, we can hardly alter that first-hand judgement. We become attached to certain settings and remain alienated in other kinds of settings, and both intuitive choices are equally difficult to verbally analyze or alter.

THE EXISTENTIAL VALUE OF ATMOSPHERE

The existential value of the diffuse but comprehensive grasping of the general ambience of a spatial entity, or an entire landscape, is rather easy to understand from the point of view of survival. It is evidently an evolutionary advantage to be instantly able to differentiate a scene of potential danger from a setting of safety and nourishment. Let me repeat, such judgement cannot be consciously deducted from details; it has to be grasped as an intuitive reading based on a "polyphonic" grasp of the ambience. This polyphonic perception and cognition has also been identified as one of the conditions for the creative mind.[7] I suggest that the elementary idea of perception, imagery and thought is altogether questionable, if not altogether wrong. In my view, this also applies to architecture and architectural education.

Our innate capacity to grasp comprehensive atmospheres or moods is akin to our capacity of imaginatively projecting the emotively suggestive settings of an entire novel as we read it. When reading a great novel, we keep constructing all the settings and situations of the story at the suggestion of the words of the writer, and we move effortlessly and seamlessly from one setting to the next, as if they existed prior to our act of reading. Indeed, the settings seem to be there ready for us to enter, as we move from one scene of the novel to the next. Yet, they are all entirely products of our personal imagination.

EXPERIENCE, MEMORY AND IMAGINATION

These processes of literary imagination are discussed in Elaine Scarry's recent book *Dreaming by the Book*. She explains the vividness of a profound literary text as follows: "In order to achieve the 'vivacity' of the material world, the verbal arts must somehow also imitate its 'persistence' and, most crucially, its quality of 'givenness'". It seems almost certainly the case that it is the 'instructional' character of the verbal arts that fulfils this mimetic requirement for 'givenness'".[8] This authority of "givenness" seems to be lacking in much of contemporary architecture aspiring for idiosyncratic and personal expression. In order to impact our existential sense, the building must exist firmly in the material and causal "flesh of the world," to use a notion of Maurice Merleau-Ponty. Czech writer Bohumil Hrabal points out the concreteness of our literary imagination: "When I read, I don't really read: I pop up a beautiful sentence in my mouth and suck it like liqueur until the thought dissolves in me like alcohol, infusing my brain and heart and coursing on through the veins to the root of each blood vessel."[9] An embodied reality is equally an essential property of architecture.

The most amazing feature of our mental acts is the synthetic completeness of our imagery. As we read a great novel, we create the urban or landscape settings as well as the buildings, spaces and rooms, and feel their ambience without, however, being able to focus on any of their details. Undoubtedly, the totality dominates the detail.

Experiencing, memorizing and imagining spatial settings, situations and events always engage our imaginative skills; both the acts of experiencing and memorizing are embodied acts in which embodied imagery evokes imaginative imagery. Recent studies reveal that the acts of perception and imagining take place in the same areas of the brain, and consequently, these acts are closely related.[10] Even perception calls for imagination, as perceptions are not automatic products of our sensory mechanisms; they are also essentially creations and products of intentionality and imagination.

In his projects and built work, Prescott Muir projects the same concerns as in his writing. Instead of gradually developing a strict and narrowing personal vocabulary, syntax, and ambience, he has chosen to explore varying points of departure. The early influence of Mies van der Rohe tends to demand a basic structural and modular principle which is locally varied. Muir enriches the classical Miesian language through a spatial and volumetric dynamism, breaking the closed and singular mass (particularly, the roof is often liberated as a hovering plate), skew elements, and a rich material palette.

Muir creates distinct and appropriate atmospheres in his projects, such as domestic, institutional and workplace atmospheres, which associate the chosen architectural language with the nature of the activities taking place within the spaces.

Prescott Muir explains his architectural balancing act between determinism and chance, deliberation and improvisation, predictability and serendipity as follows:

> "Our work has endeavoured to provide a platform for engagement that transcends in an assertive way the nearsighted science of sustainable technologies on the one hand and the infinitely adaptable rhetorical surface treatments on the other. Unlike the post-structuralist critique that each act of will invariably is accomplished at the expense of another rendering all acts irreconcilable and thus equivalent, I propose an architecture based upon simple acts of observation and measurement or what Niels Bohr calls registration that can be accumulated while allowing adjustments and assemblage in a cloud of probability where certainty and uncertainty may coexist. The response to a certain instance or instrumentality derived from simple observation does not necessarily preclude other options and may invite serendipity. This is not an architecture of absolutes yet does not close out its possibility and thus noticeably veers from the historical utopian origins of Modernism and its provocations.[11]

Even in the beginning of the third millennium, the task of architecture is to strengthen our existential foothold on earth. Buildings, cities and other man-made structures continue to provide us our most significant horizons of perception, understanding and meaning. And it is the poetic dimension of buildings alone that can project lived and existential meanings.

JUHANI UOLEVi PALLASMAA

Juhani Uolevi Pallasmaa is a practicing architect, educator and theorist with his own firm, Arkkitehtitoimisto Juhani Pallasmaa KY, located in Helsinki, Finland. He has contributed to and authored over 34 books, including the recently published The Embodied Image. His Book, *The Eyes of the Skin,* has become required reading in architecture schools worldwide and occupies the libraries of most prominent architects. He maintains a demanding international schedule of exhibiting, guest criticism and lecturing. He is a professor emeritus at the Helsinki University of Technology, past Director of the Museum of Finnish Architecture, Honorary Fellow of the American Institute of Architects and holds visiting chairs at Washington University (St. Louis) and the University of Illinois Schools of Architecture.

1. In my view, architectural works can be reliably judged only through an actual live encounter. Buildings address our entire bodily being and existential sense rather than the eye or any other sense modality, and meanings arise decisively from the dialectics of the landscape and the building, context and scale, materiality and light. Even the journey to the site may be a significant part of the narrative and layering of meaning. As I enter a building, I subordinate my body to an exchange; the space becomes part of me, and I project myself onto the space.
   As I have not had a chance of visiting buildings designed by Prescott Muir, I must limit my comments on his architectural designs to observations which I can deduct from photographs, i.e. remarks on conceptual rather than experiential characteristics.

2. Prescott Muir, "Clouds, Clowns and Distorting Mirrors," manuscript for an essay, 2011, p. 1.

3. Peter Zumthor, *Atmospheres – Architectural Environments - Surrounding Objects*. Birkhäuser, Basel, Boston, Berlin, 2006, p. 13.

4. Sir Colin St. John Wilson, "Architecture – Public Good and Private Necessity," *RIBA Journal*, March 1979.

5. Robert Pogue Harrison, *Gardens: An Essay on the Human Condition*. The University of Chicago Press, Chicago and London, 2008, p. 130.

6. Zumthor, op. cit., p. 13.

7. Juhani Pallasmaa, *In Praise of Vagueness: diffuse perception and uncertain thought,* manuscript for a book on psychoanalysis and architecture to be published by the University of Texas, Austin, Texas, 2011.

8. Elaine Scarry, *Dreaming by the Book*. Princeton University Pres, Princeton, NJ, 2001, p. 30.

9. Bohumil Hrabal, *Too Loud a Solitude*. Harcourt, Inc., San Diego. New York, London, 1990, p. 1.

10. Ilpo Kojo, "Mielikuvat ovat aivoille todellisia [Images are real for the brain]." Helsingin Sanomat, 16.3.1996. The article refers to research done at Harvard University under Professor Stephen Rosslyn.

11. Muir, op. cit., p. 4.

WALKING THE LINE
A REFLECTION ON THE WORK OF PRESCOTT MUIR
by Dan Hoffman

THE PUBLICATION OF A MONOGRAPH on the work of Prescott Muir is a welcome and long anticipated event for the design community, an opportunity to assess the work of this important architect and consider its place in the ongoing development of modern architecture in the western region of the United States.

Muir has had an active practice in Salt Lake for 35 years and has made significant contributions to the architectural culture of the region through the design of a wide range of building types including private residences, urban housing and institutional buildings. The large majority of the projects are located in and around Salt Lake City, Utah, a city with a strong tradition of urban planning dating back to the Mormon settlements of the 19th century but lacking strong, home-grown examples of contemporary architectural design. This could be due in part to the Mormon tradition that emphasizes planning, functionality and economy over visual, aesthetic concerns. The mining industry, long prevalent in the region, has left a legacy of robust industrial buildings that have also influenced the culture of building. The landscape is dominated by the basin and range geography prevalent in the inter-mountain west region, juxtaposing raw rock cliffs and the evergreen forest of the mountains with the semi-arid grass covered basin. The presence of the mountains with their ever-changing play of shape, color and shadow might also be a reason for the lack of a strong architectural tradition in the region, with buildings taking a back seat to the dramatic views of the surrounding mountains. As with other cities of the region, such as Phoenix and Las Vegas, the Salt Lake area is growing rapidly, but unlike Phoenix, with its distinctive desert climate and emerging school of desert architects, the Salt Lake region has not yet developed a unique, regional style.

Muir's highly nuanced and introspective work is a remarkable exception, demonstrating how a singular commitment and passion for the Modernist architectural tradition can gain traction and begin to inform the cultural sensibility of a place. In this way he is part of a tradition of modern architects working in the coastal and intermountain west regions that have emerged in the post-War era, applying Modernist design principles in inventive ways that highlight the landscape and material culture of their particular locales.

A number of these architects are now emerging on the national stage, applying their sensitivity of local influences and building traditions to the overarching formal narratives of Modernism, bringing a new vitality and relevance to the Modernist trajectory. Architects such as Wil Bruder in Phoenix, Miller-Hull in Seattle, and Morphosis in Los Angeles have enriched their respective communities with their works, creating vital, local schools and movements based upon their work.

These architects understand that Modernism is not simply a style, but rather, a process of design that frames local circumstances within a universal, geometrically based syntax that allows for invention through the incorporation of local building materials and craft traditions.

The tradition of West Coast Modernism began in Los Angeles with Richard Neutra and Rudolf Schindler, followed in the post-War period by Case Study architects. Taken together this group translated the intellectual and formal precepts of European Modernism into an American, Modernist tradition. As noted above, the formal Modernist tradition is built upon the idea that architectural form is geometrically determined, and as such, lends itself to what the philosopher Husserl termed as an "idealizing praxis," an application of technology towards an ever more refined and precise manifestation of pure, geometric form. In other words, modern architects embrace technology as a way to render built form in more precise ways. Edges and planes become straighter, flatter and thinner, and the articulation of volumes and solids more hollow and uniform. Modern architects were fascinated by thin, resistant qualities in modern building materials such as glass and metal panels, and their ability to create an ambiguous relationship between indoor and outdoor spaces. Structural components of the buildings were reduced to thin frames which were often painted black to emphasize their precise, linear qualities. The light, open feel of these structures, captivated a generation of modern architects and established the Modernist principles of lightness, openness, flexibility, invention and construction as emblematic of the post-War generation. From a formal perspective, their compositions were informed by formal principles of the dynamic balance of forms in a two-dimensional figure ground context as demonstrated in this painting by Hans Hoffman. These principles were used to organize both the floor plan and elevations of the building, allowing architects to respond to complex, asymmetrical conditions found in their sites and programs. The late work of Rudolf Schindler as represented by the Mackey Apartments (now the MAK Center) is perhaps the most vigorous and dynamic example of this compositional approach, creating a façade that both separates and binds together the individual apartments in a single structure.

Mackey Apartments—Rudolf Schindler

Hans Hoffman

These principles were reinvigorated in the 1970s and 1980s through the work of American artists Donald Judd, Richard Serra and Robert Irwin, who critically examined the perceptual experience inherent in Modernist composition, taking it out of the two-dimensional realm of painting and into the sculptural world of bodily movement. The art object now

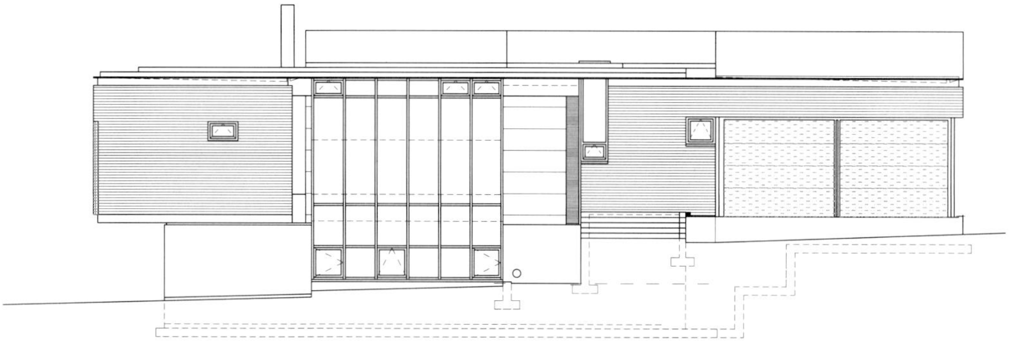

16'

South Elevation
Michigan Avenue Residence, Salt Lake City, Utah

engages the viewer in a perceptual dialogue, weighing an ever-changing perceptual understanding of the object against a conceptual model or idea of how it is constructed or formed. These artists were also interested in the inherent material qualities of an object, expanding the field of structure through the use of materials used in architecture and heavy construction such as concrete, glass, rusted steel and aluminum.

It was inevitable that architects would incorporate these phenomenal lessons into their work, engaging the inhabitant more deeply and critically in the experience and nature of the building. During this period, architects expanded their palette of materials to engage their buildings more directly with the natural context. Will Bruder was one of the first to incorporate this approach in his work, juxtaposing the colors of qualities of rusted metal and glass against the bright light and shadow of the stark desert landscape.

It should be noted that despite the interest in the phenomenal qualities of material, architects continued to deploy neo-plastic compositional strategies to organize their plans and elevations. This is clearly in evidence in Prescott Muir's recently completed Michigan Avenue house. Here the composition is articulated by overlapping planar surfaces, each defined by its own material, brick, black curtain wall glazing, flat aluminum panels and stucco. As with the colors in the Hoffman painting, the relative intensity and value of the building materials enhance the layered, spatial reading of the façade, causing the surfaces to be read in front of or behind the other. The planes of material also give an indication of the spatial organization of the house, with its central living space flanked by the master bedroom suite and kitchen dining areas. The central hall is a recurring organizational motif in Muir's work, recalling the Mormon meeting halls typical of the region. The difference, however, is in the asymmetrical articulation of the plan with its subtle spatial overlapping and stitching between the central space and the flanking elements. Muir has refined this compositional play over the years, marking each move on the interior with a corresponding move on the exterior, creating a refined, legible architecture for those who take the time to observe carefully.

The fine-tuned attention to detail and calibrated composition can also be found in Muir's elegantly constructed drawings, which provide the reader with an insight into Muir's compositional technique. Here we see the architect carefully calibrating the composition, weighing the thickness of a mullion against the proportion of a window opening located on another portion of the wall, aligning the placement of a door with an opening on the other side of the room. The precision and care of these drawings is remarkable, each line revealing a material and spatial insight into the project. Unfortunately, the tradition of two-dimensional architectural drawing is quickly being replaced by 3D computer renderings marking the end of a long tradition and possibly the end of the Modernist fascination with the refined production of layered geometrical space.

Muir's interest in facades reveals a sensitivity and commitment to a traditional urban street wall context. This makes him unique among the second-generation West Coast Modernists who tend to view their buildings as singular constructions that are meant to be perceived from multiple vantage points. The list of Muir's urban buildings is impressive: the Rose Wagner Performing Art Center, the Bridge Mixed-Use Project, the Salt Lake City Arts Center and Ballet West Conservatory, which all underscore the architectural contribution that he has made to the urban design of the region.

The Rose Wagner Performing Arts Center is as close as Muir has come to employing typological precedents on his facades, a step away from Modernist abstraction. Given the large size of the planned project (the master plan calls for an adjacent theater that will double the size of the building on the street), Muir was challenged by the requirement of creating a block-long building wall with few windows or ground-floor openings in an emerging arts district with active streets. This was achieved much in the same manner as the Michigan Avenue house, by creating a rich material palette that defined the programmatic zones of the building while creating a sense of depth within the shallow façade. Punched windows, framed ground floor openings and a notional entablature give a contextual nod to the bearing wall typology of the surrounding historic buildings while a selection of modern materials and motifs, such as diagonal struts supporting a thin projecting eave atop the building wall and metal-clad street, level volumes, animate the façade. The taut street wall is broken in dramatic fashion by a large opening framed with steel beams, creating a deep, proscenium-like arch framing the main circulation stair within.

One of the most intriguing of Muir's urban projects is the proposal for the Swaner Nature Preserve Building. Located at the edge of new town center in Park City, Utah, the site looks out onto a large, wetlands/meadow surrounded by the peaks of the Wasatch Range. The building was to house an ecological center dedicated to the preservation of the natural habitat of the region while serving as visitor's center trailhead for a raised pathway into the wetlands/meadow. Muir's response to the site is illuminating and profound. Instead of opening the view of the wetlands/meadow from the interior of the town center, Muir takes the bold step of blocking the view with a long blank wall perched atop a row of thin columns, which also serves to conceal the functions of the visitor's center from view of the town. Curiously, elements of the building clad in white appear and peek out from behind the floating wall. To further confound the visitor, horizontal slit windows peer out from the wall like the half-closed eyes of a sleeping animal. What can be made of such a bold, urban gesture in this rural setting?

Upon reflection, the blank wall is a dramatic gesture that conceals the anticipated scene from view while heightening the anticipation of the viewer for what is to come, the thinness of the wall enhancing the sense of depth beyond. Gaston Bachelard has noted that the apparent depth of the ocean is made even more profound when peering down through the water of a flat placid sea. In a similar way, the depth and space of the meadow and its surrounding mountains are made more profound through the presence of the wall that serves both as a whole in the middle of the scene as well as thin, opaque surface against which the sense of depth is registered. Maybe this was all too much for Park City, Utah.

Few architects of the region would attempt such a bold act of negation. However, to paraphrase Henri Bergson, the negative is inherently a richer condition since it assumes the positive *and* its negation.

CANYON RESIDENCE

The Canyon Residence is one of the more accomplished and expressive of Muir's works. Set into the side of canyons flanking Salt Lake City, the house engages with the context in bold and nuanced ways, using a wide array of formal moves and material effects. A departure from the frontal organization of Muir's urban work, the Canyon Residence demonstrates his ability to work in a variety of Modernist genres and measures up to the best work of his regional colleagues, such as Will Bruder in the Southwest and Miller-Hull in the Pacific Northwest.

The house captures the rugged and variable nature of the basin and range landscape typical of the region, with its rugged peaks, canyons, grass-covered foothills and flat plains. It also captures qualities of the industrial remnants of mining towns that dot the region, precariously perched on steep hillsides with their rusted metal shacks and black-painted steel gantries.

Unlike the Michigan Avenue house, with its taught, urban façade and precisely balanced relationship to the slope, the Burgess Residence engages in an expressive dance with the landscape, with one wing of the house buried into the upward slope of the canyon while another projects over the downward slope and floats lightly over the garage and arrival plaza. Another comparison with a work of Hans Hoffman helps to illuminate how the formal Modernist vocabulary is adapted to looser, more dynamic ground plane. His painting of 1959, entitled *The Gate,* loosens the interlocking geometry of the figured fragments, allowing the bright, precisely painted rectangles to float free above of the green painted ground, which flows around the space of the painting, pushing up against and falling away from the precisely rendered rectangles. In some instances the dark green reads like a shadow, giving volumetric weight to the spatial ground of the painting. Similar spatial effects occur in the Canyon Residence with the shadows created by the lifted roof and receding garage doors above and below the blue-tinted glass walkway and the dark blue pool set into the rear stone terrace. The range of material and light effects are remarkable, adding dynamic, phenomenal qualities to Muir's rich compositional palette. The play of light, material and space continues in the interior of the house. Dark stone and steel fireplaces punctuate the space from the ground up as colored shafts of light cut through the ceiling, illuminating cabinets of wood, glass and metal. As with the Michigan Avenue residence, the plan is divided into three zones with a large living and dining room flanked by a bedroom wing and master suite. However, as with the massing of the house, each part is given its own unique material and spatial quality.

Given the formal complexity and range of phenomenal qualities manifested in the Canyon Residence and the strides that it has taken from the works of the early West Coast Modernists, it is interesting to speculate on the next phase of the Modernist trajectory. Will the geometric rigors of the "idealizing praxis" hold as new materials and techniques allow architects to continue to refine the phenomenal qualities of geometric form? Will formal strategies continue to evolve along the Cartesian (rectangular) path, or will new, inflected geometries take hold? Will architects continue to design "from the ground up," inspired by the natural and cultural qualities of the places where they live and work? The depth and breadth of Muir's work provides many opportunities to weigh these questions. Future generations will have much to learn from how it deepens and energizes the understanding of a place through the dialogue it constructs between global intellectual currents and the nature and history of a region.

DAN HOFFMAN
Dan Hoffman is a practicing architect, urban designer, educator and published theorist. Hoffman is a principle, and co-founder of Studio Ma, the award-winning collaborative design studio located in Phoenix Arizona. Several noteworthy projects include the Student Housing at Princeton University, the Salt River Sustainability Center, the PRD Infill Housing and the Entry Portals to the Cranbrook Campus. He is the former Head of the Department of Architecture at the Cranbrook Academy of Art and has taught at the University of Detroit, University of Toronto, University of Michigan and Arizona State University, with visiting positions at Yale, Texas, Waterloo, Cornell and Illinois universities. Hoffman is currently a Clinical Professor in Practice at the University of Utah School of Architecture. He has lectured and exhibited his work internationally at over 60 schools. He is widely published andhis book include *The Architecture Studio* by Rizzoli Press.

PERMEATE

CANYON RESIDENCE
Salt Lake City, Utah

When exposed to nature, building materials decay at different rates, which provide opportunities for design. Just like the human body, that absent surgical intervention over time provides an imprint of experience and behavior reflected in the contours of skin. The Canyon Residence location in the steep canyons overlooking the Salt Lake Valley, affords a direct engagement with nature not always found in the city. The severe desert sun on the western horizon in the summer has always been a challenge and conundrum for the development of the city with primary views that face this direction. Also, during the winter months for houses located in the canyons, the sun barely rises over the canyon rim, thus impeding access to direct sunlight for months at a time.

The house was built for a couple and their teenage children and needed to anticipate the transformation of the family dynamic in a very short period to entertain alternative uses while defining integral relationships with the site and vistas beyond that are static and predicable. The design is a series of cantilever living spaces anchored to the hillside with deep recesses oriented to the west. The building is suspended over earth-bound stone walls that incorporate cor-ten steel plates within the coursing which provide a different rate of erosion from the stone itself, one informing the other as an acceptance of time. This graceful engagement with entropy is a skill that architects have forgotten.

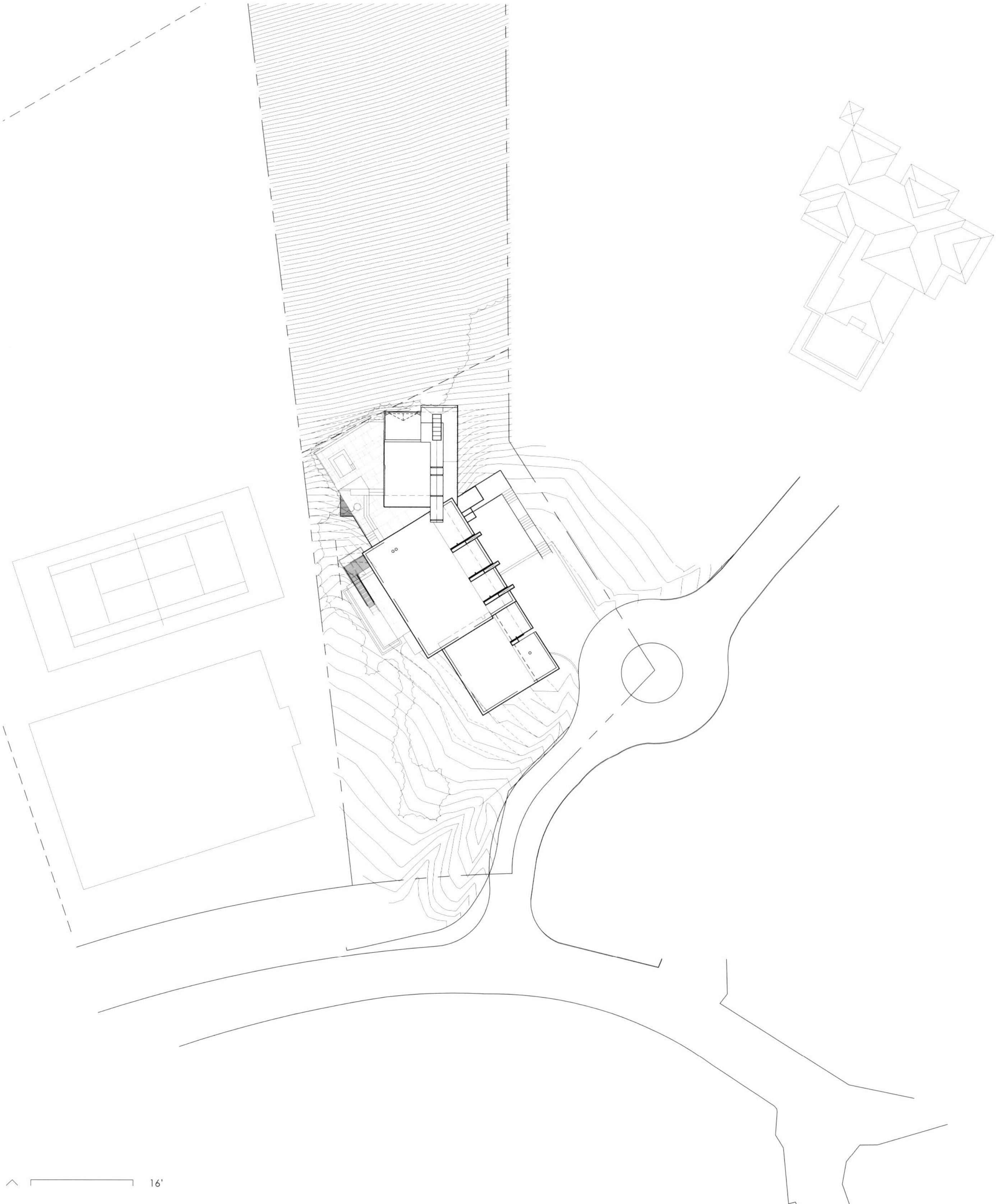

Site plan

30

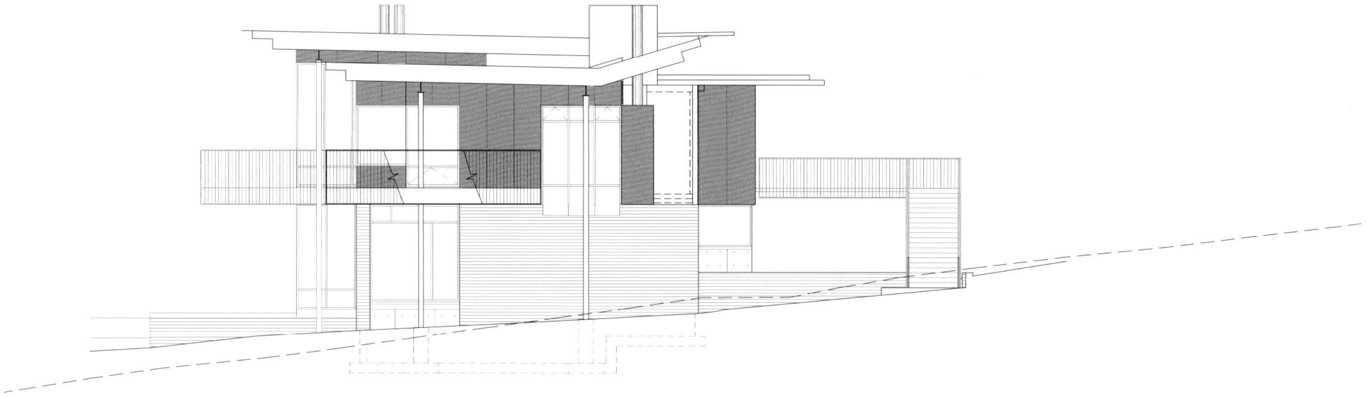

South elevation

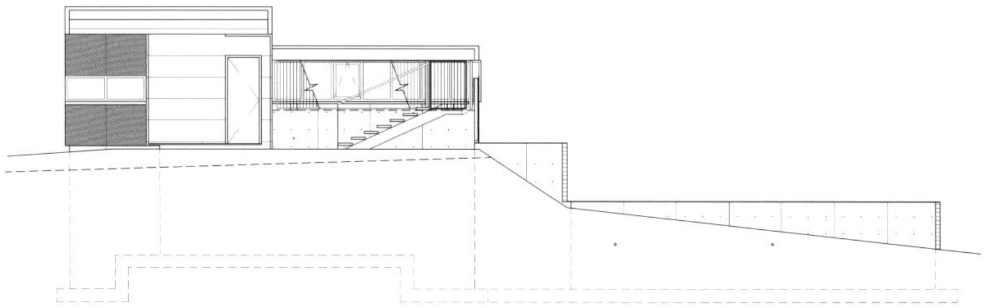

North elevation

16'

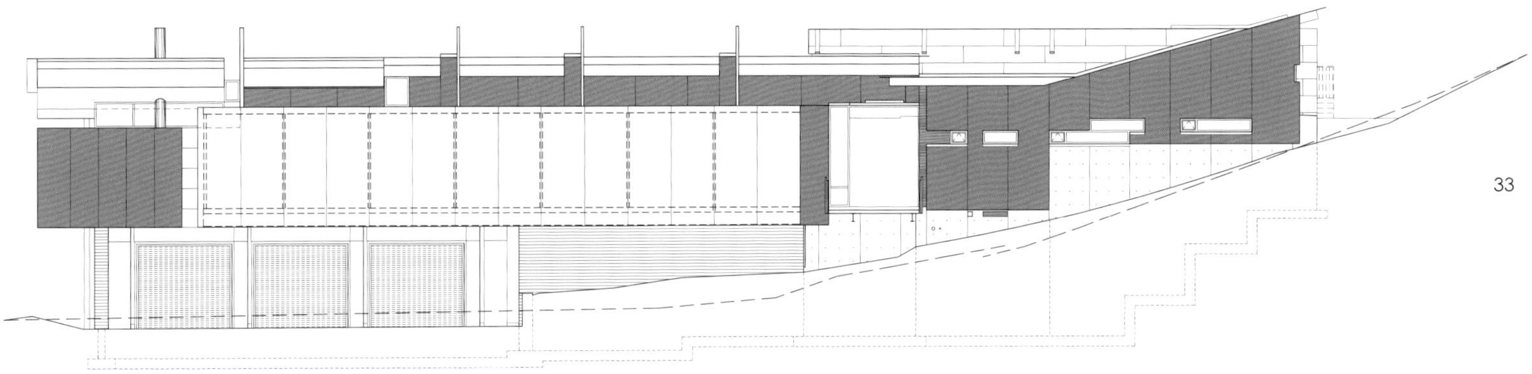

East elevation

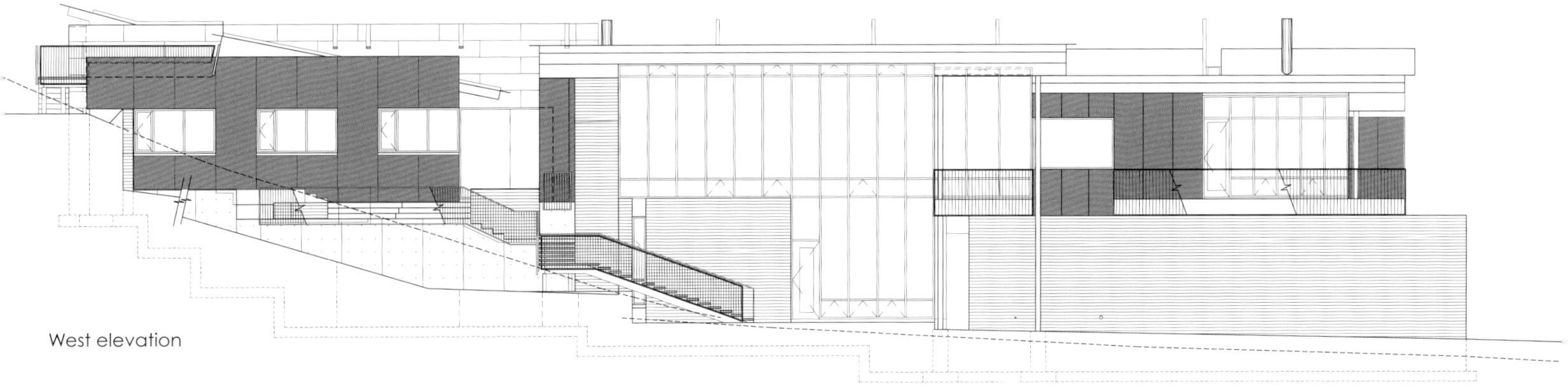

West elevation

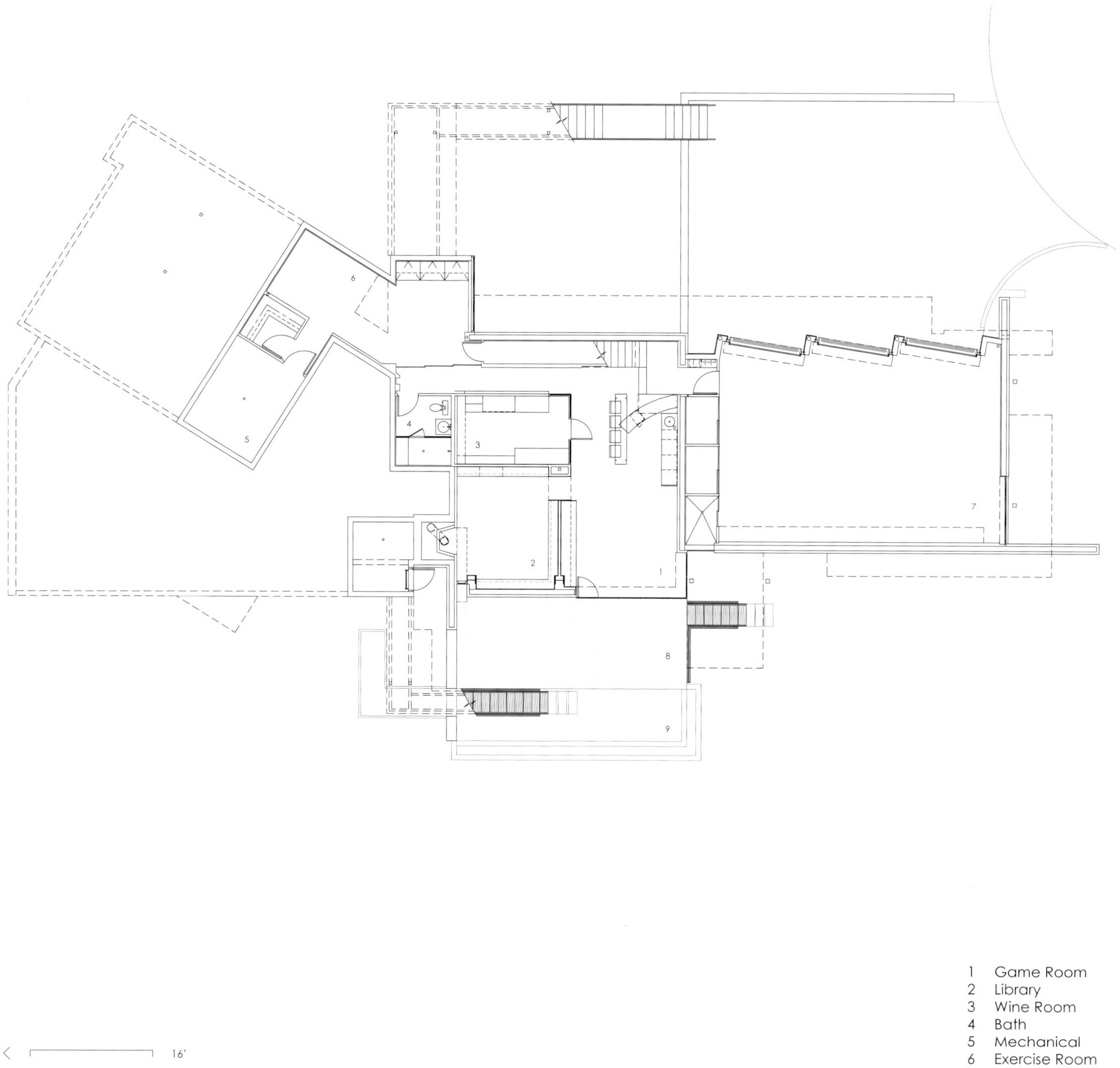

First floor plan

1 Game Room
2 Library
3 Wine Room
4 Bath
5 Mechanical
6 Exercise Room
7 Garage
8 Patio
9 Reflecting Pool

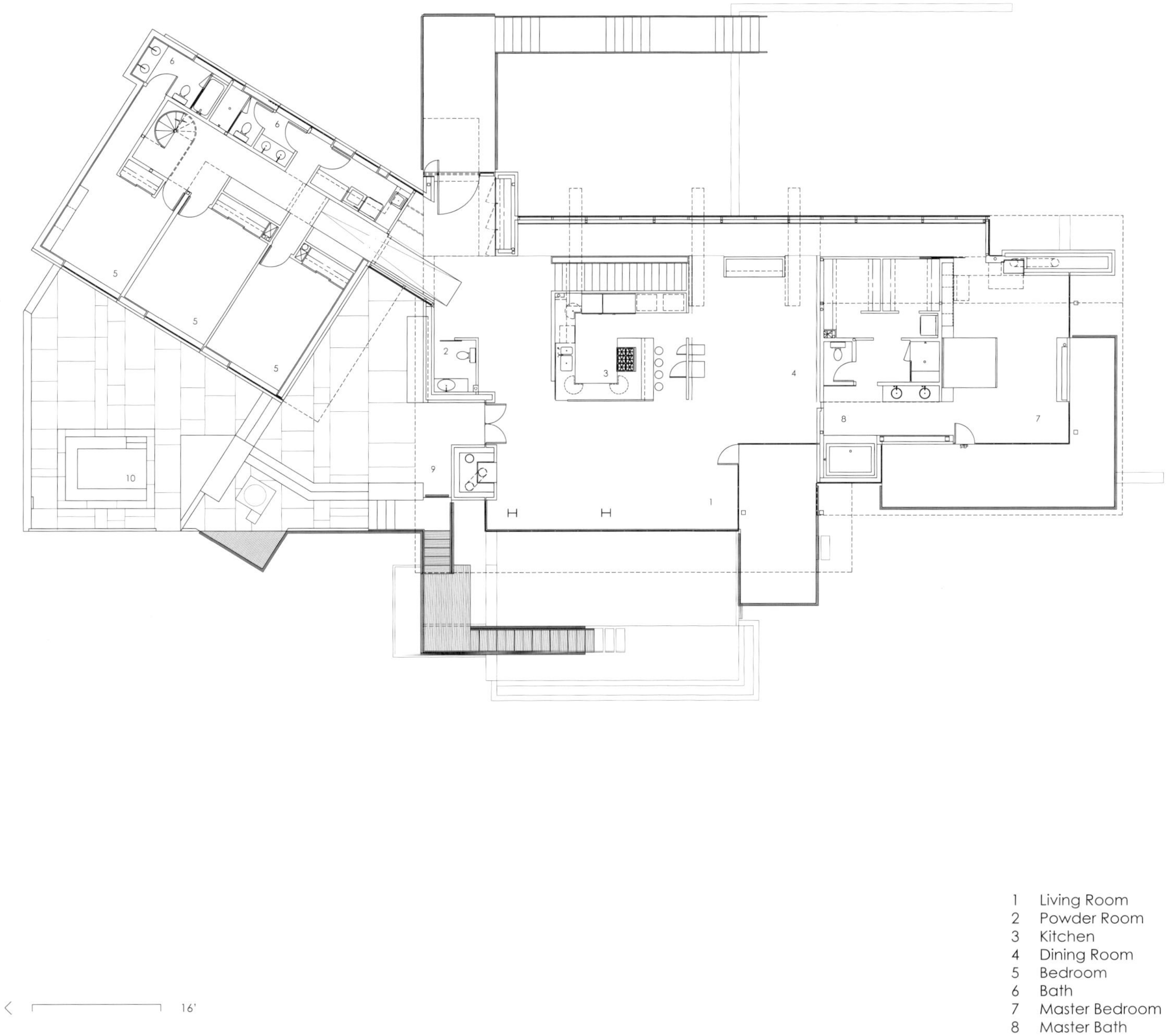

1 Living Room
2 Powder Room
3 Kitchen
4 Dining Room
5 Bedroom
6 Bath
7 Master Bedroom
8 Master Bath
9 Patio
10 Spa

Second floor plan

ALTA RESIDENCE

Alta, Utah

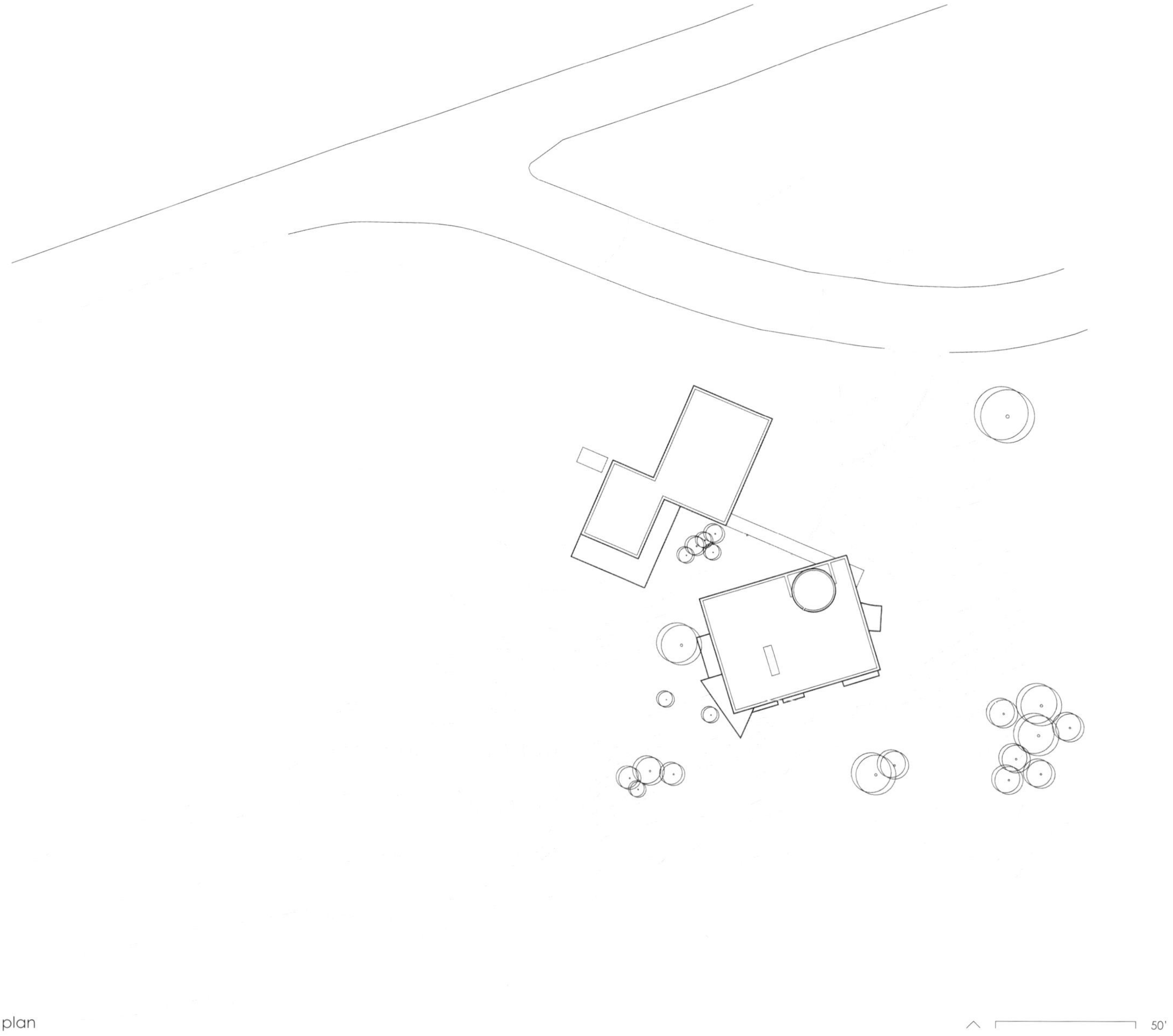

Site plan

Alta is a place of striking beauty, but contained in that beauty is the latent threat of severe weather conditions, with hundreds of inches of annual snowfall and corresponding avalanches. As a consequence, buildings must respect both extremes: the serenity of the summer landscape and its reciprocal conditions. The house is positioned at the edge of a rugged stone cliff from which it emerges with a precision-cut stone base and transitions to a sleek if not taut concrete envelope. The simple lines of the concrete act to bind and limit the structural envelope. Like a primitive cliff dwelling, the house is closed to the uphill exposure and opens towards views to the south that coincides with the leeward side of any potential avalanche impact. The stair tower enables light to drift down through the interior of the house, delicately illuminating the suspended staircase contained therein. The centrifugal array of balconies and mud room imply the suppressed potentialities of this site.

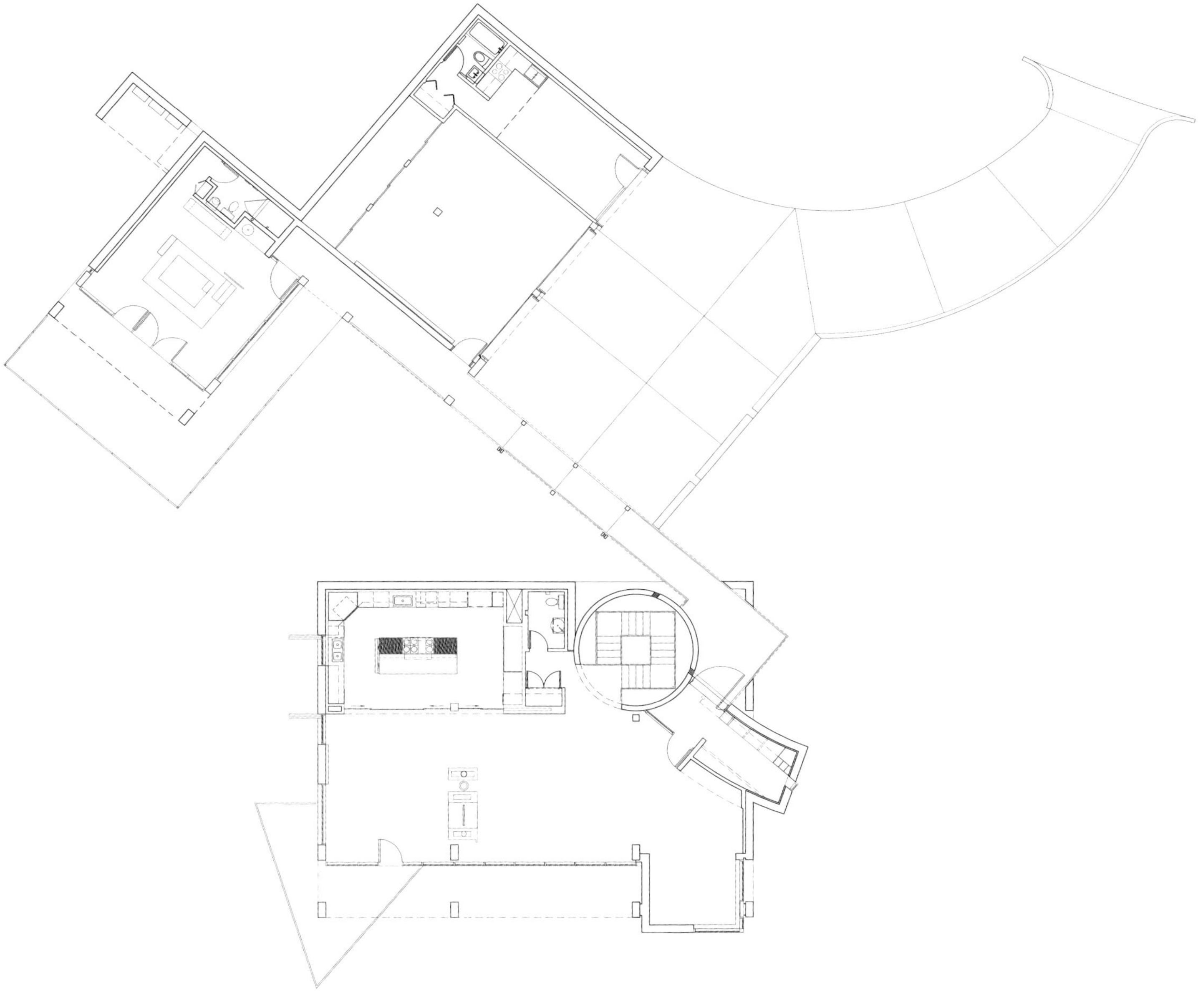

Third floor plan

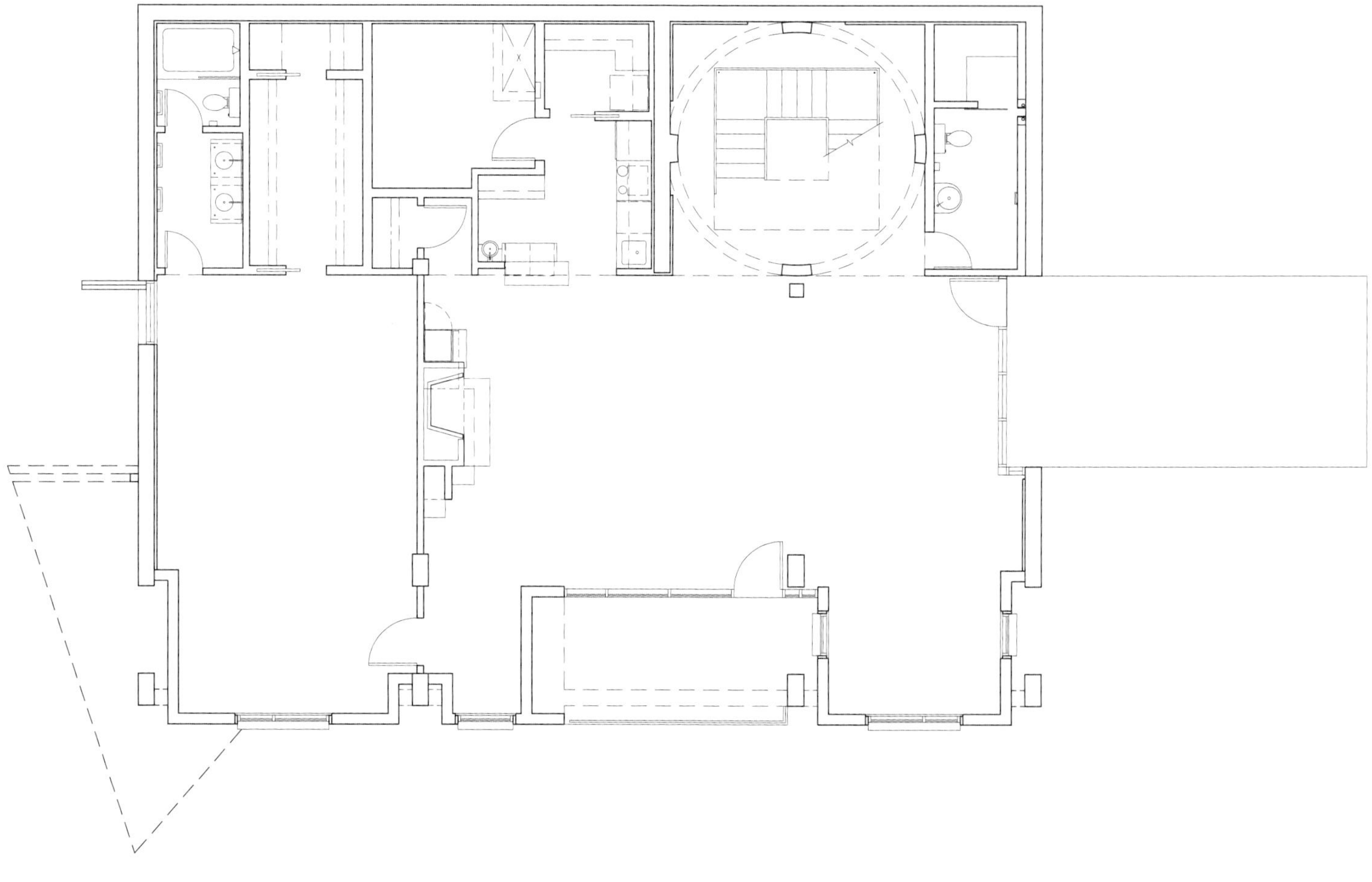

16'

First floor plan

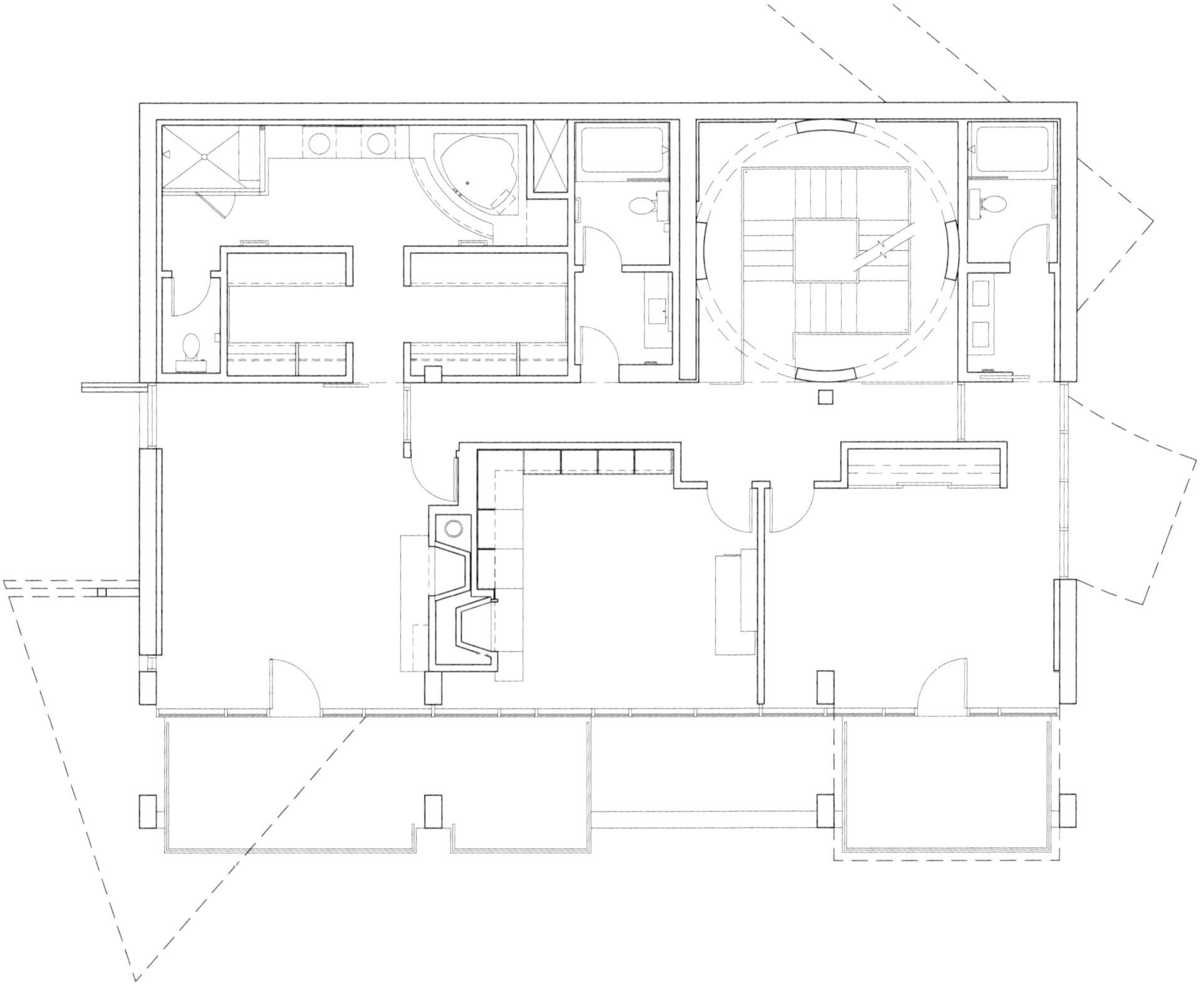

16'

Second floor plan

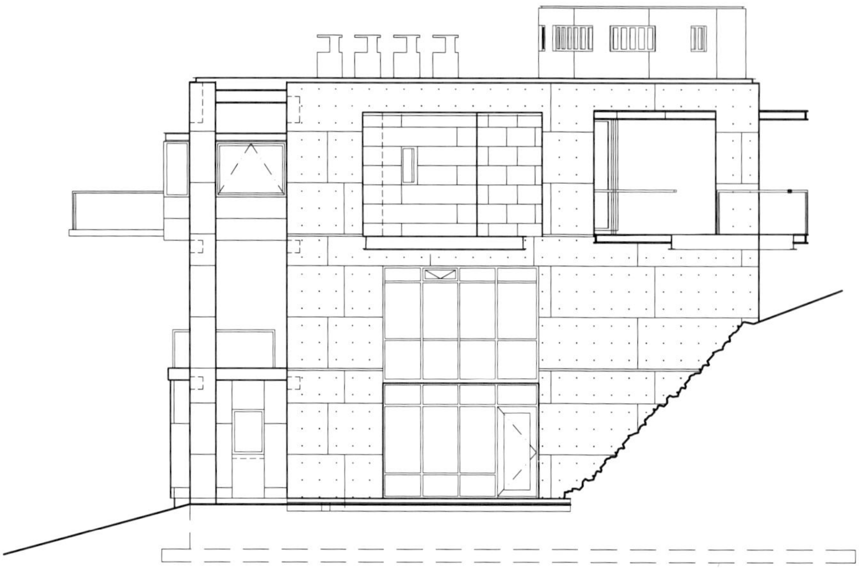

East elevation

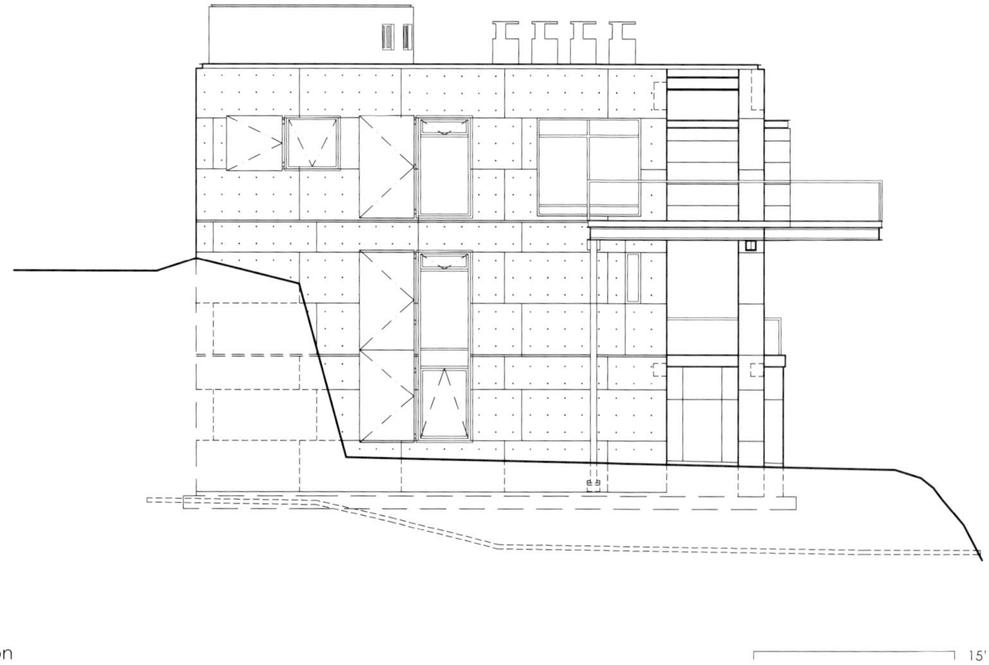

West elevation

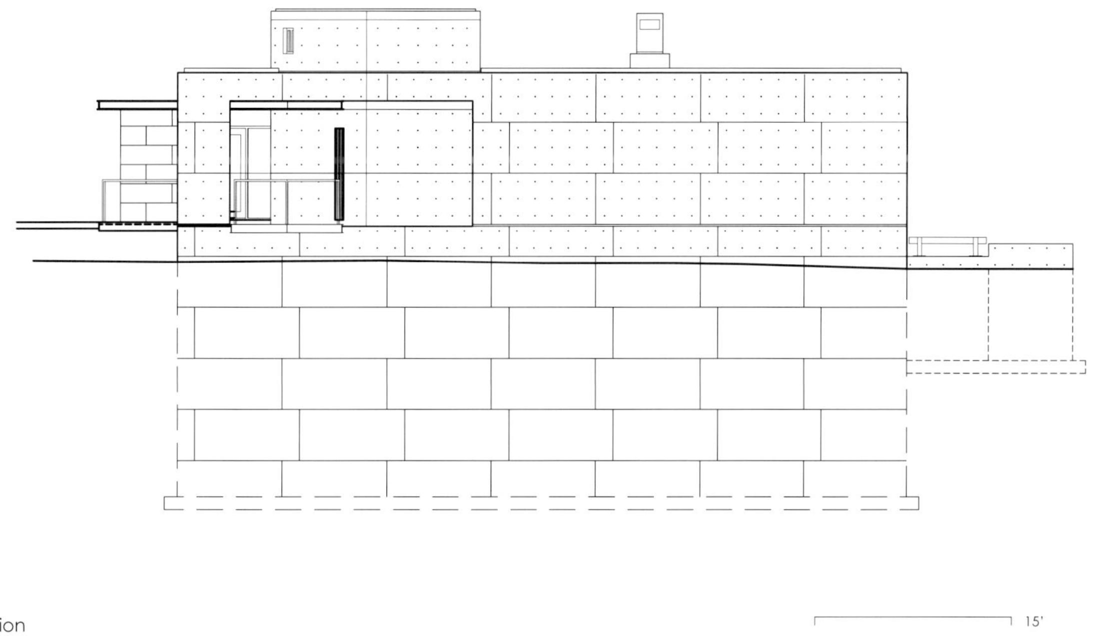

North elevation

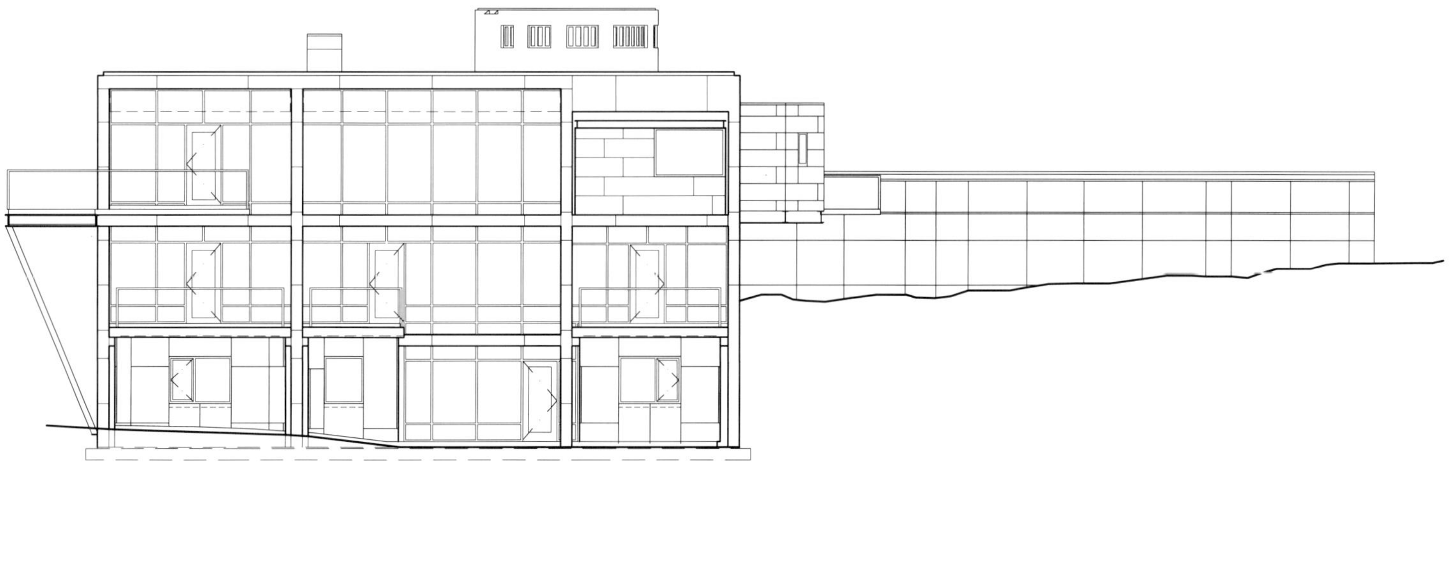

South elevation

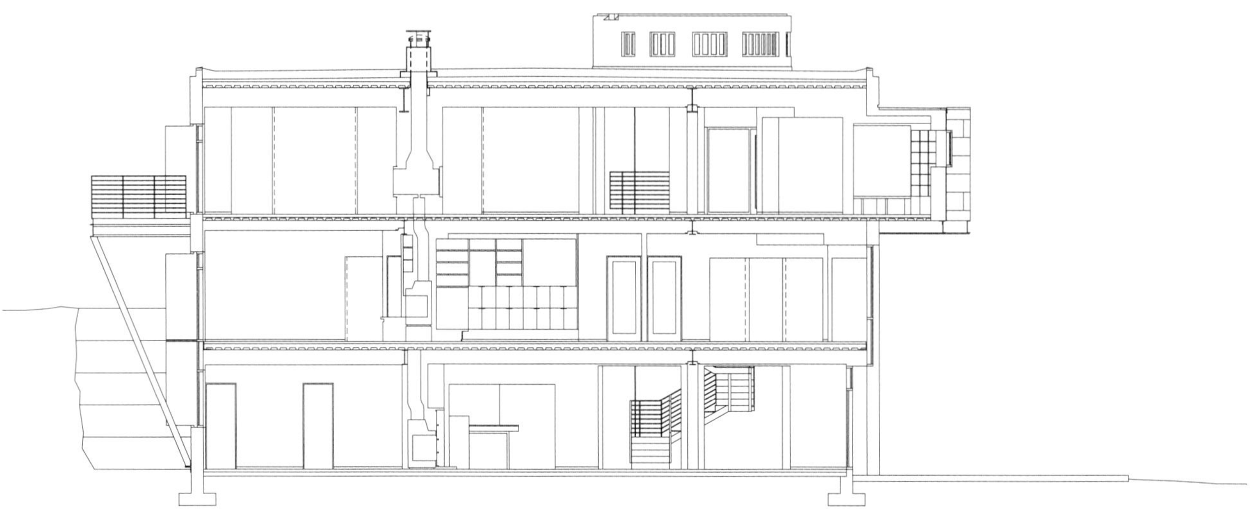

North section

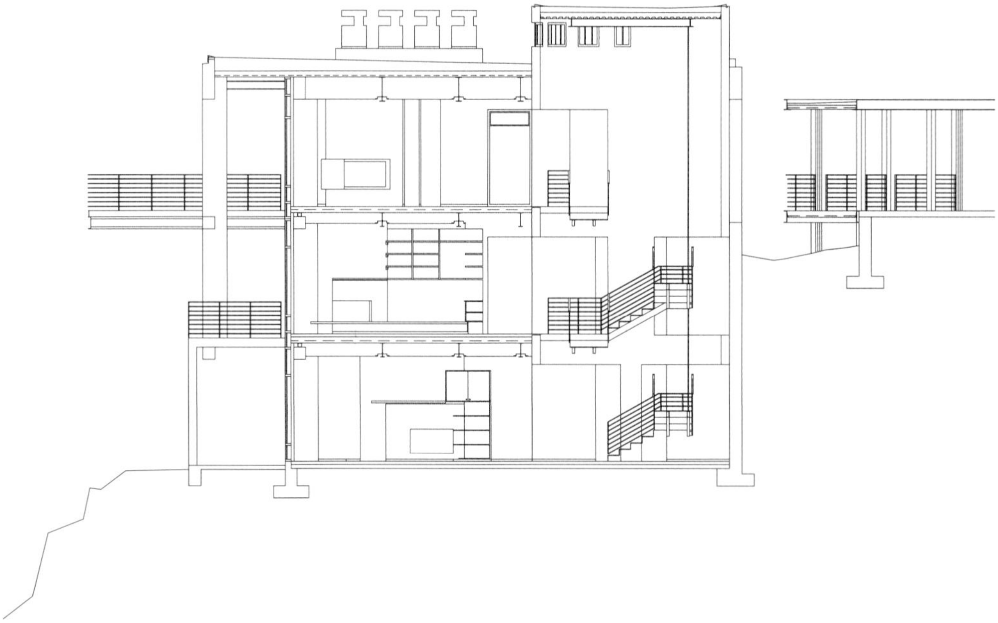

West section

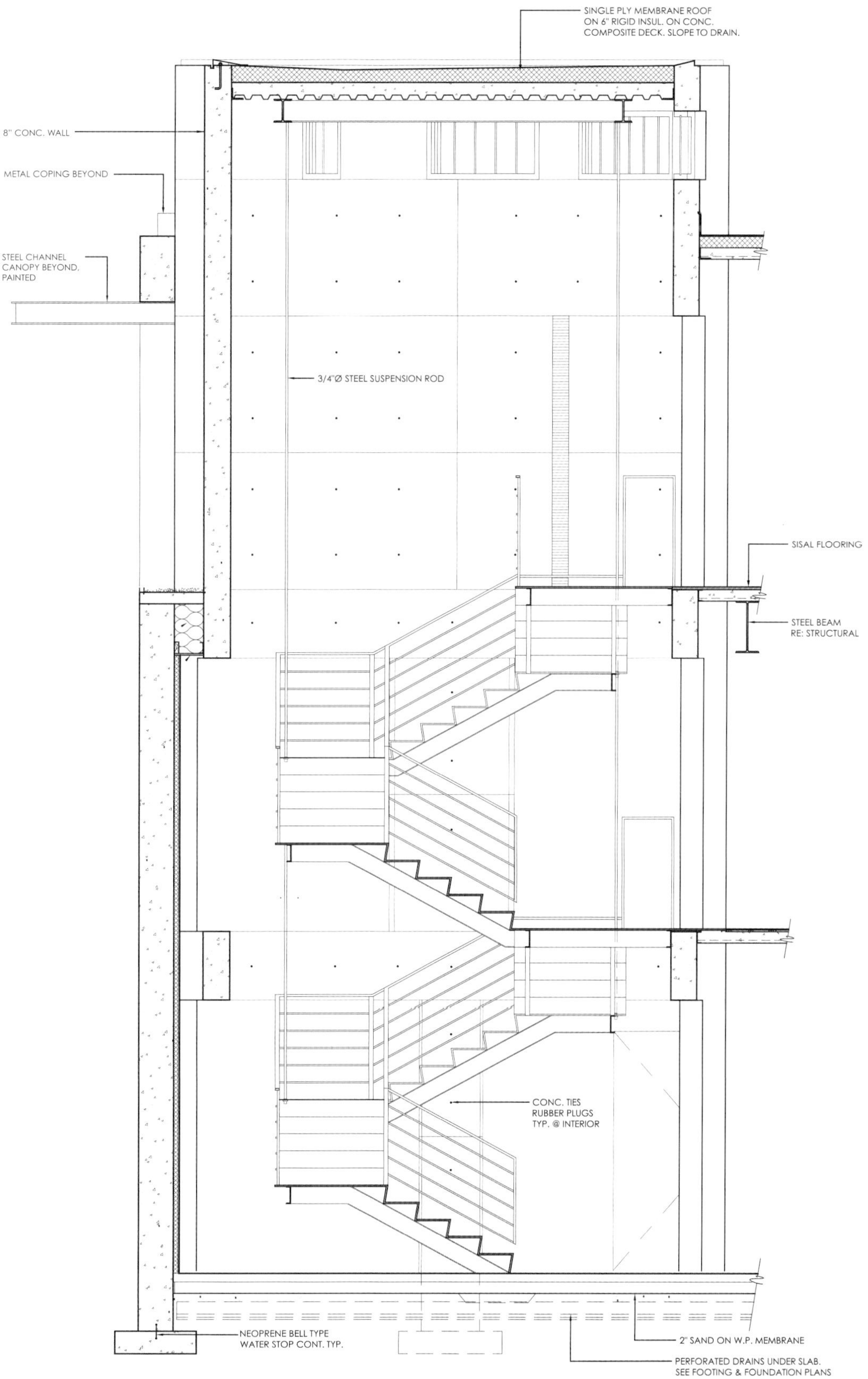

Stair section

6'

WEBER COUNTY LIBRARY

Pleasant Valley Branch
Washington Terrace, Utah

LIBRARY

Washington Terrace is a suburban area only differentiated by its proximity to Hill Air Force Base and the path for F16 jets as they fly over the site in radical trajectories. A library is a building that implies a centripetal configuration, with the security of a main reading room that welcomes contemplation and offers escape in a book or computer screen. As the initial orientation point for new immigrants and visitors to the community, the library needs to provide implicit way-finding and a welcoming presence. The building provides discrete windows placed around the reading room and art gallery so that the passage of time is clearly recognized and marked by direct sunlight that traces the room's perimeter. The landscape is cropped by discrete views as though they were pictures on the wall, thus allowing the central space gravitas as a room with clearly defined limits.

Character is derived from the simple fact that roofs need to slope to drain. There is no need to look elsewhere to find meaning. Given the dynamics of the site, with vapor trails marking the sky, sonic booms and imposing mountain peaks, a library seems incongruous. The building construction manifests this tension between internal and external orientations with a brick bond that is offset one third and includes periodic reveals that become visible as armatures for containment and mark the passage of the sun.

LIBRARY

LIBRARY

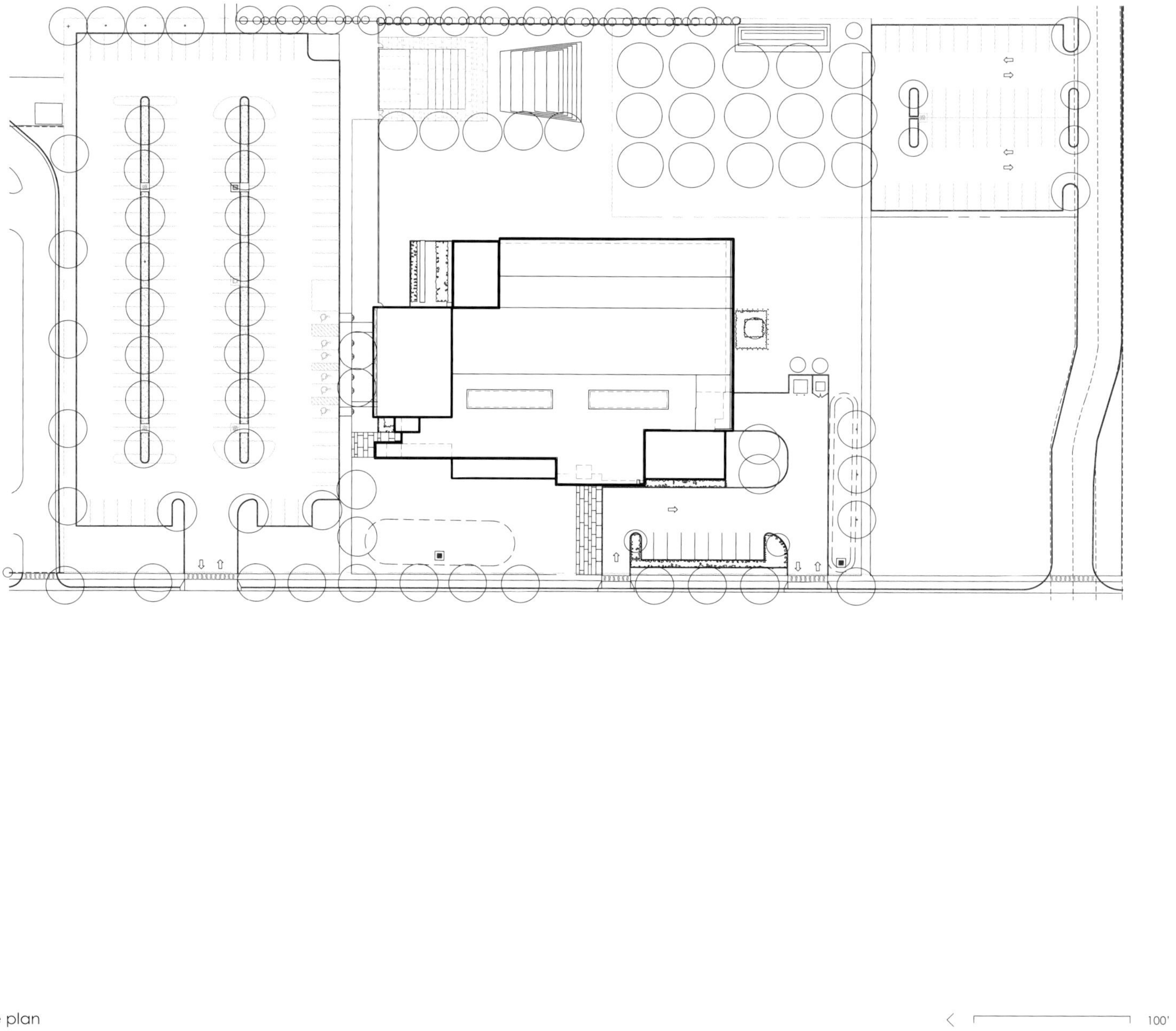

Site plan

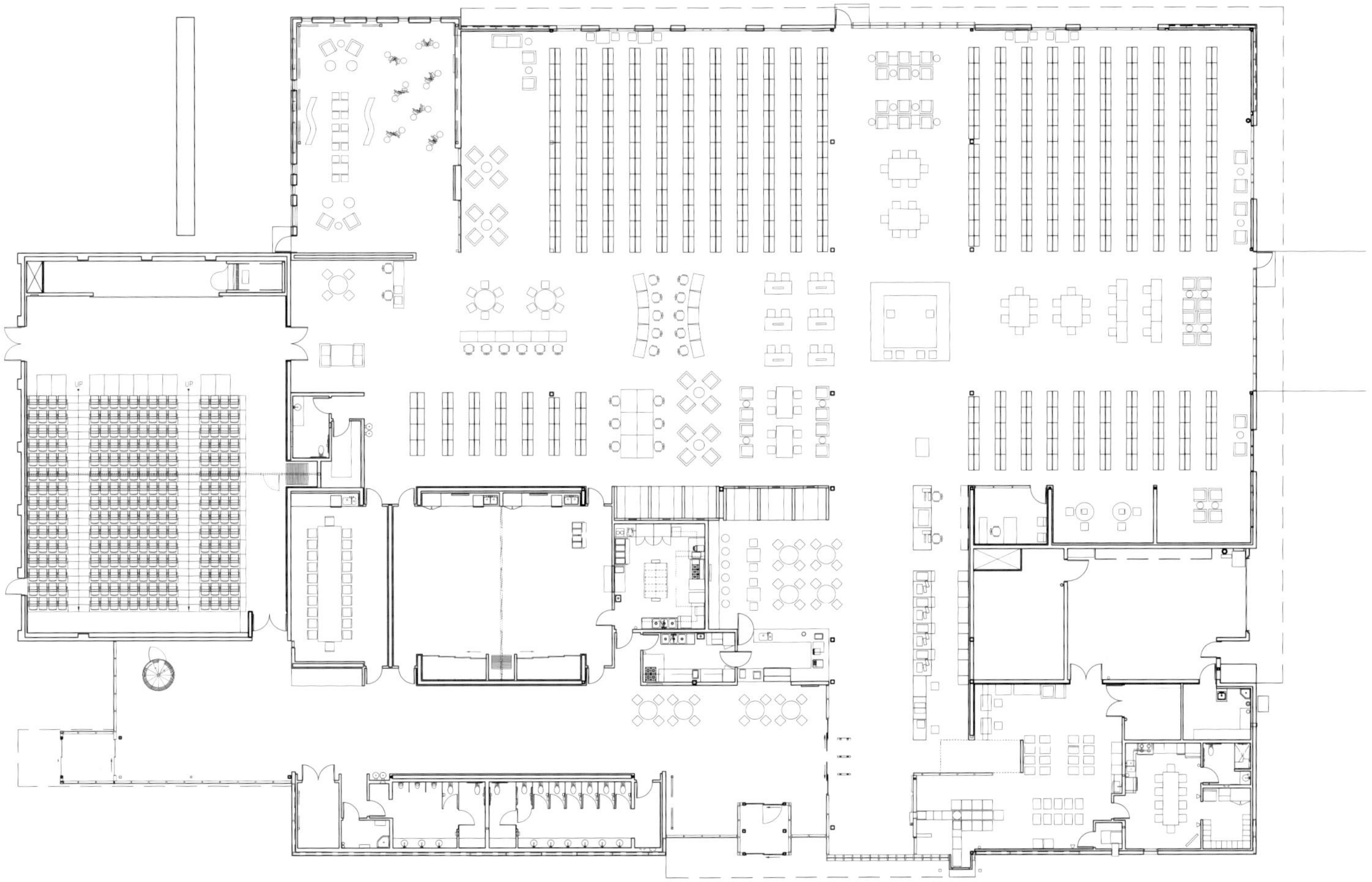

Main level

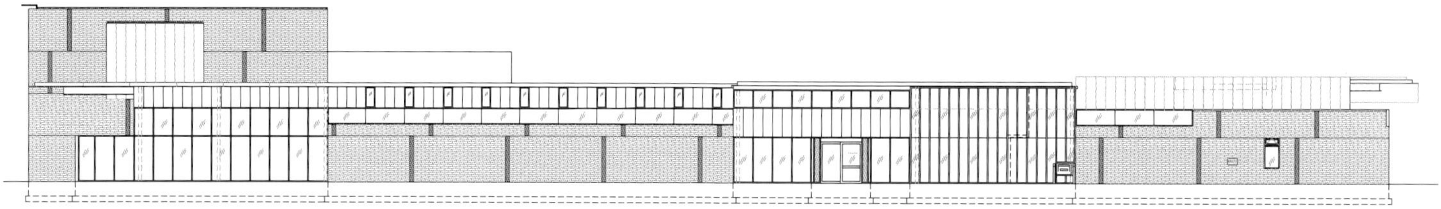

West elevation

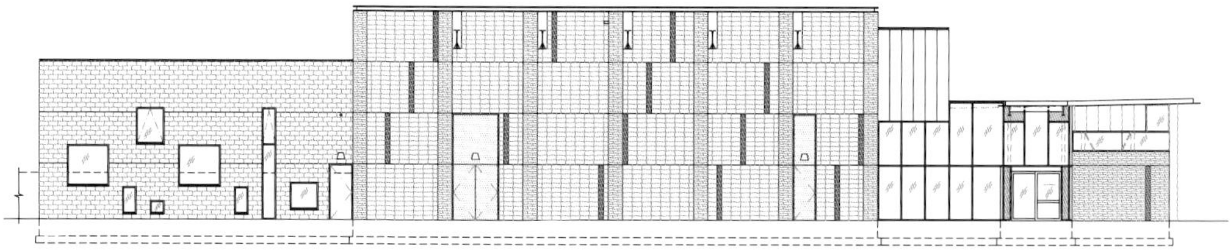

North elevation

32'

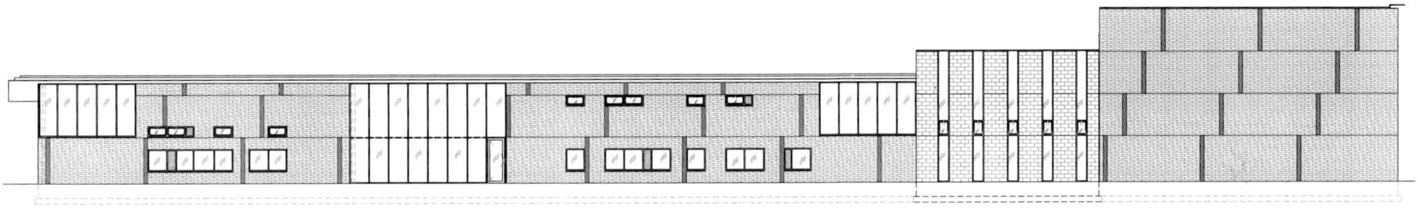

East elevation

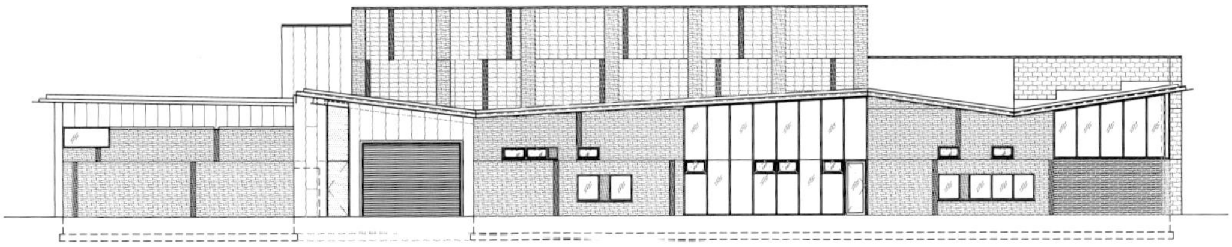

South elevation

EXIT

READ
READ

SWANER PRESERVE

Park City, Utah

86

The Nature Preserve, though located in Park City, is surrounded by suburban development and thus provides an oasis of subtle grass land and habitat for mostly small animals, birds and fish. The Preserve functions to cleanse the storm runoff as well as breathe for the built environment. We had noticed that in more rural locations the agricultural hay sheds eclipse the landscape, as though something were edited from it in a very abstract and singular way. We used this method of addition through subtraction by using an elevated plane of blackened copper to not only focus one's attention internally to the material itself but to also obscure the horizon line and focus attention to the immediate path and peripheral views. Is consciousness heightened when the visual is diminished? The building is to the Preserve as the Preserve is to its suburban context.

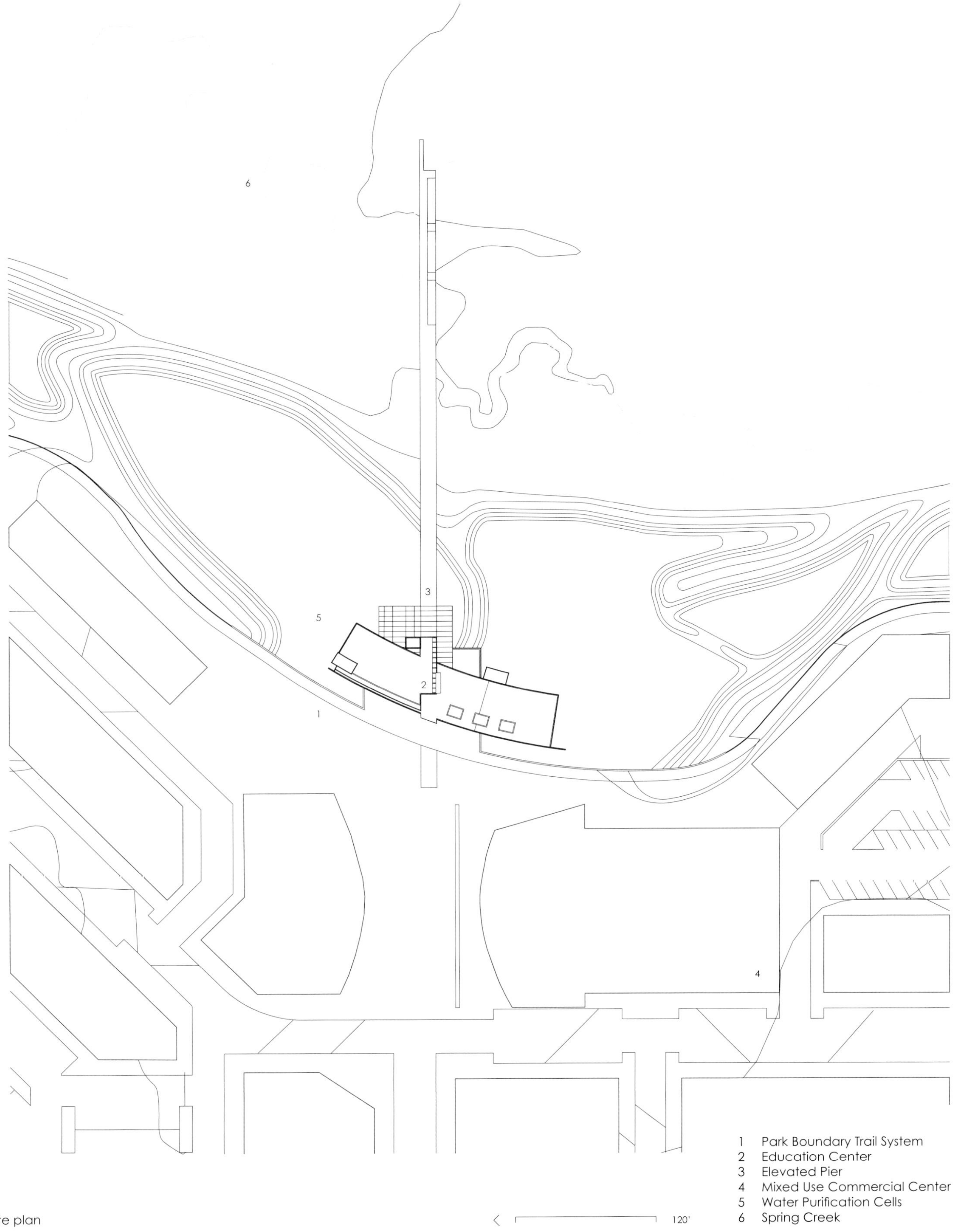

1 Park Boundary Trail System
2 Education Center
3 Elevated Pier
4 Mixed Use Commercial Center
5 Water Purification Cells
6 Spring Creek

Site plan

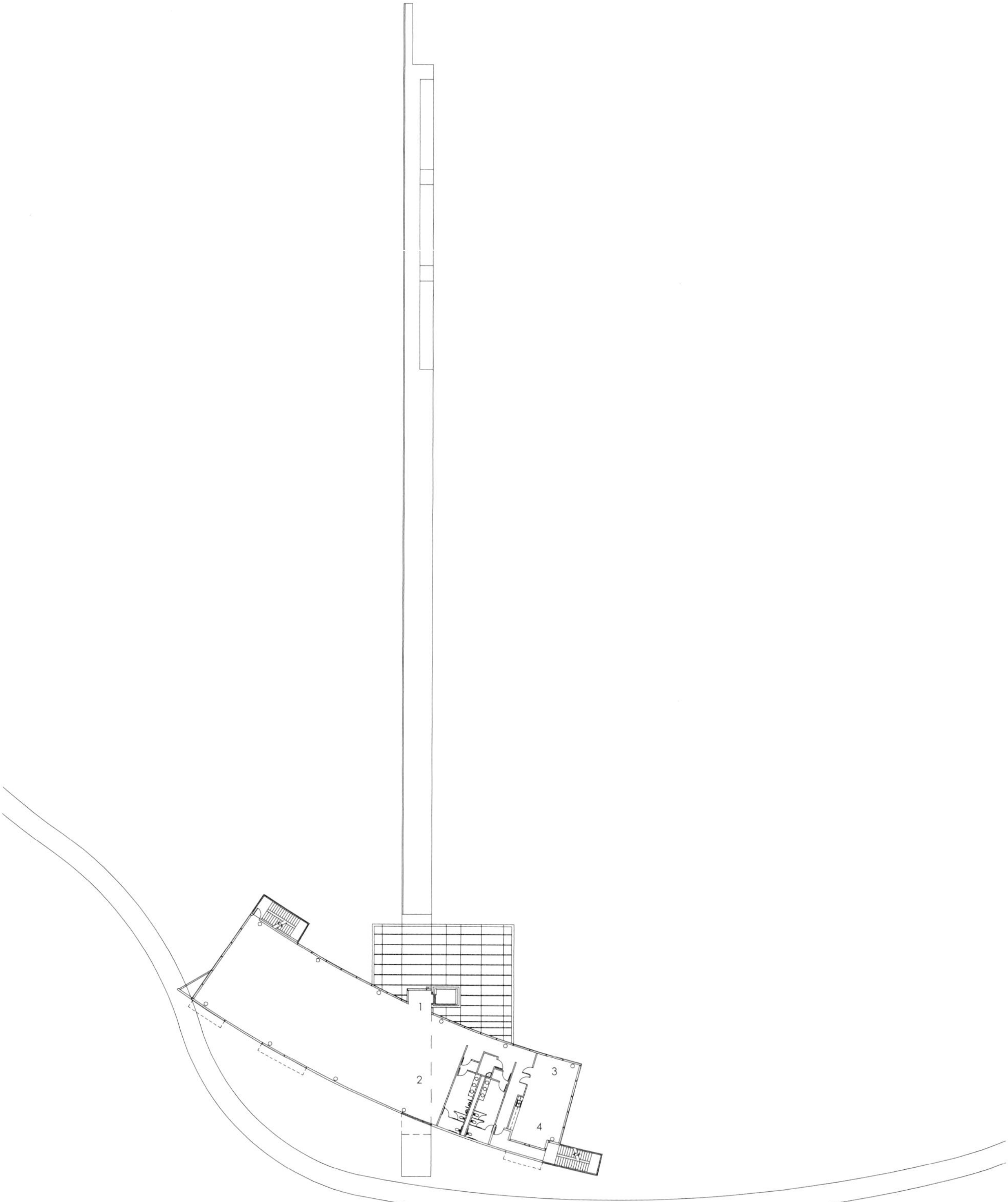

Second floor plan

1 Lobby
2 Exhibition
3 Classroom
4 Catering

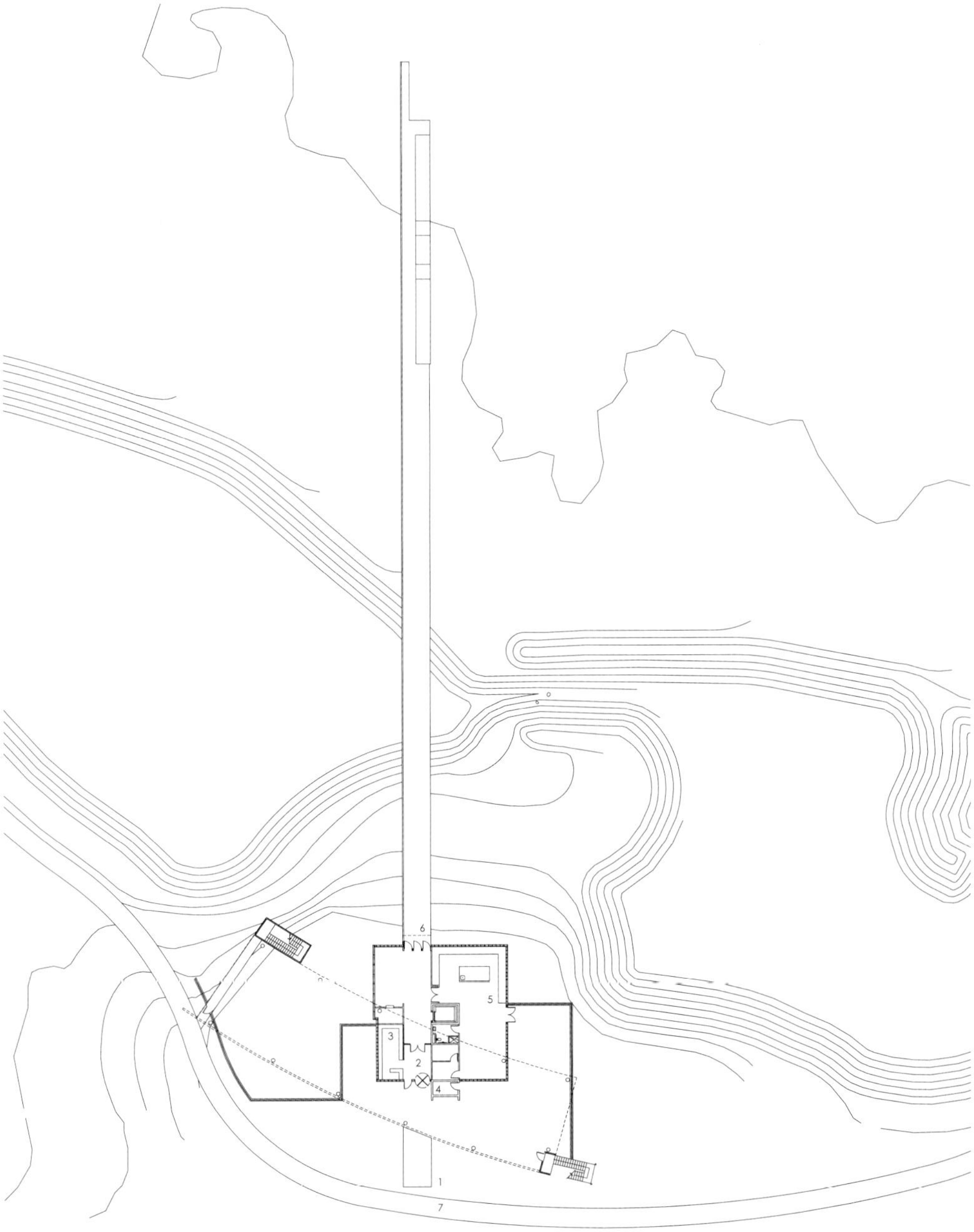

Main floor plan

60'

1 Plaza
2 Lobby
3 Gift Shop
4 Equipment
5 Green House
6 Pier
7 Park Trail

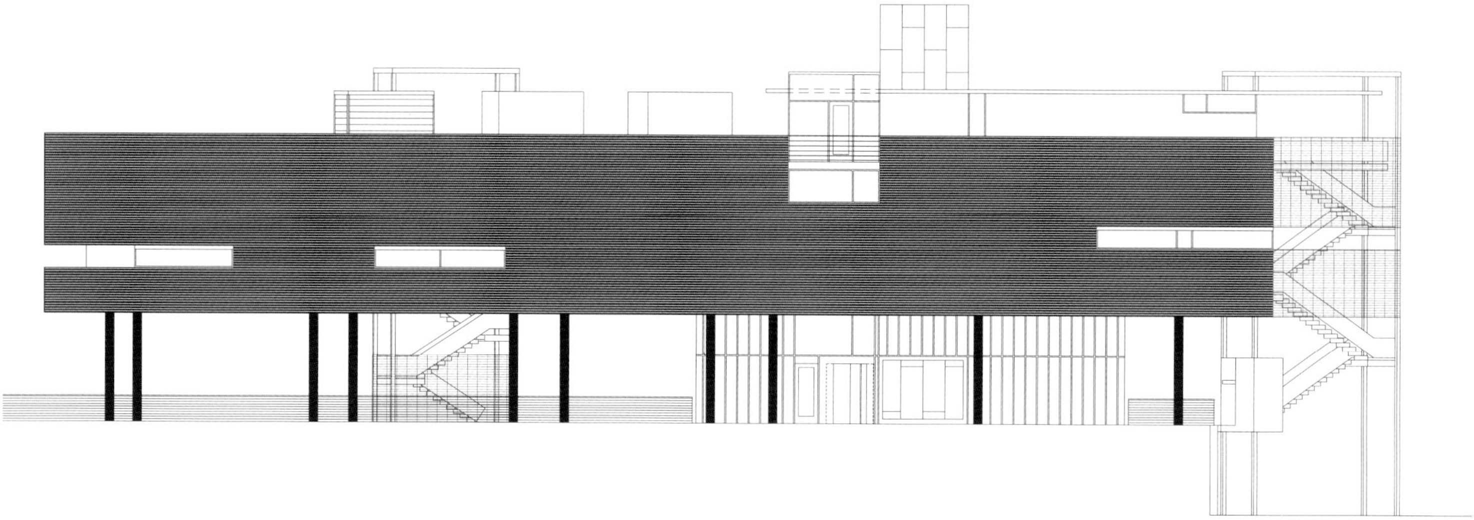

West elevation

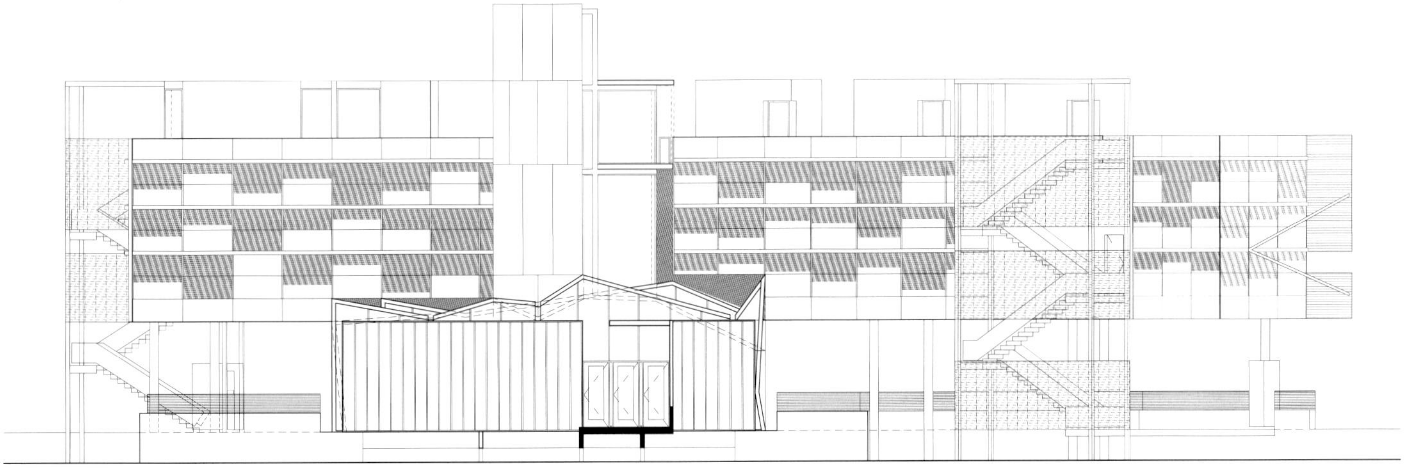

East elevation

MALIBU RESIDENCE
Malibu, California

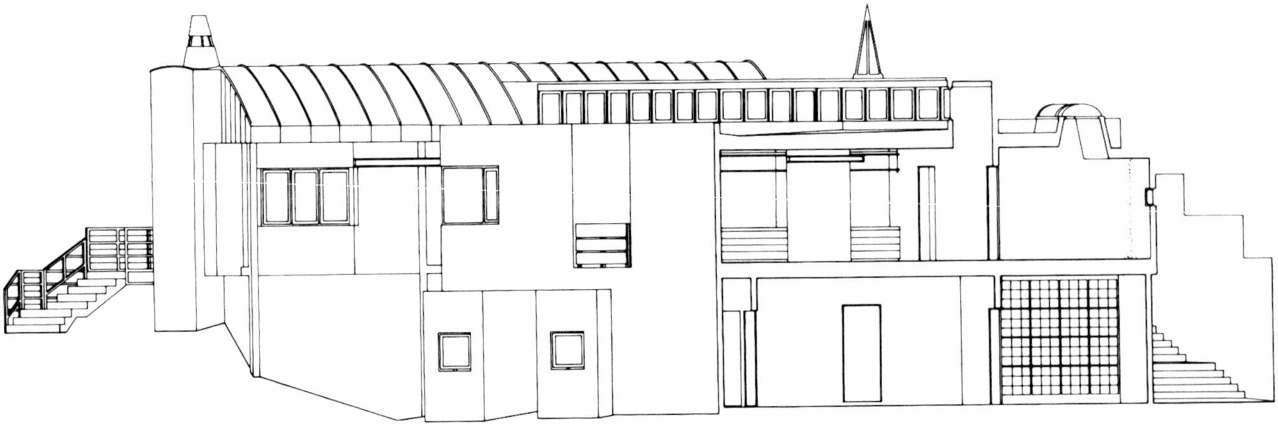

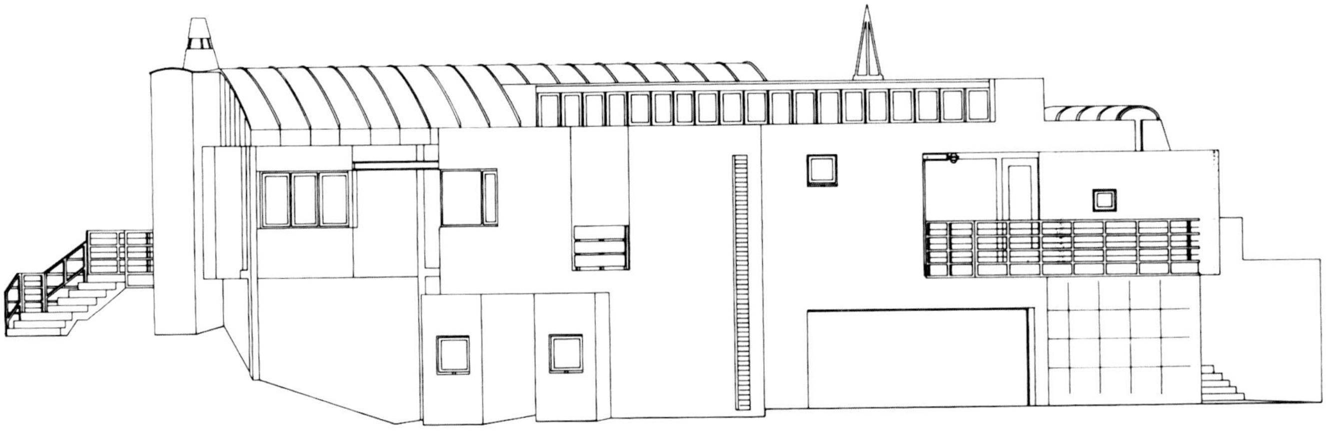

A wine merchant and his animation artist wife identified this site in Malibu Canyon for their residence and family, which included two daughters. The house, built in 1986, responds to the narrow site and western view that is captured at the brow of the hill above the point of entry from the road. The design diagram is a shifting of reference points as one traverses the slope, thus creating external points of reference. Unlike Salt Lake, where the western views are dramatic but environmentally treacherous, the western sun in Malibu is often obscured by the marine layer. Each element of the house provides personal and formal associations with each family member. The communal area is simply a large room that maximizes views and offers a central area for the family.

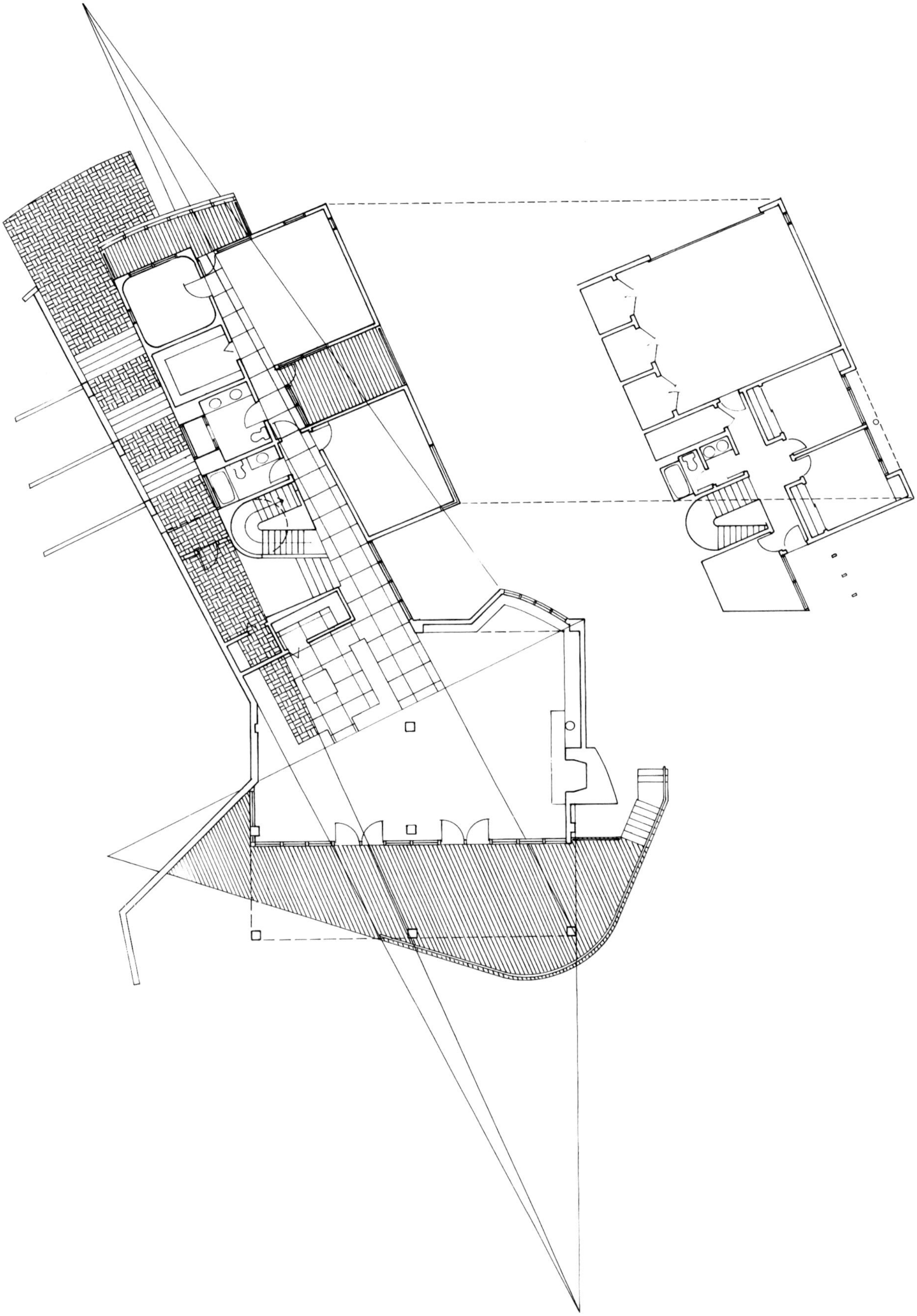

INDICATORS

CLOUDS, CLOWNS AND DISTORTING MIRRORS

by Prescott Muir

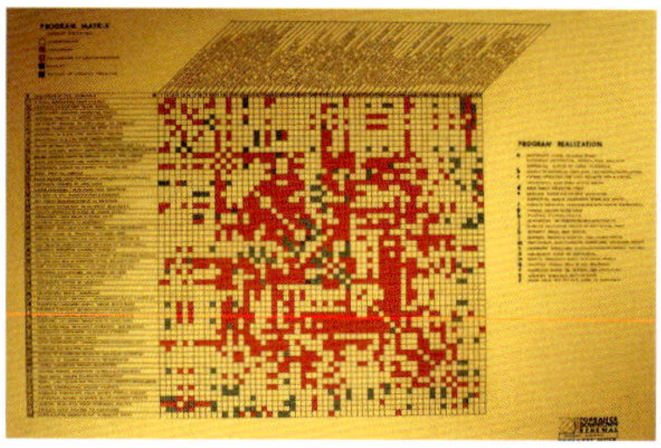

ALBERT EINSTEIN AND NIELS BOHR had a running 25-year debate about whether the universe was predictable and deterministic (as Einstein offered) or unpredictability and prone to accident (as rebutted by Bohr). This grew out of Einstein's commitment to find a global unifying theory grounded in the discovery of the singular subatomic building block upon which to explain the universe. Conversely, Bohr had a greater willingness to accept the inexplicable complexity and indeterminacy suggested by quantum mechanics. Was this an early progenitor of the post-structuralist conundrum of rhetoric versus scientific proof? Their collaborating physicist at Princeton, John Archibald Wheeler, coined the title "It from Bit" as a mediation between the two positions, envisioning a universe that in "all it contains [it] may arise from the myriad yes-no choices of measurement [bit]."[1] Yet this is a system able to yield to accident and the distorted influences of perception, thus suggesting a transcendence beyond the otherwise unequivocal positions.

Looking back, Wheeler's idea of "It from Bit" seems to me a logical extension of the ideas of Christopher Alexander that I applied in the studio while just a young undergraduate student at USC. At the time, the work of Alexander seemed like a way to reconcile the influences of determinists like Alfred Caldwell, Konrad Wachsmann, Ralph Knowles, and Ian McHarg with that of a young maverick, Frank Gehry; at that time, all of these figures were teaching at USC. Mies van der Rohe's ideas, as taught by Caldwell just two years after Mies' death, seemed restrictive, and the Modernist canon seemed calcified while Gehry's ideas were disconnected, inarticulate and lacking the refinement and subtlety of Mies. A student would be understandably confused. Could there be an element of predictability in design where you concede authorship and the trappings of ego in favor of some antonymous and indeed anonymous system as in, say, one of Breton's automatic writings? Or was design found in the liberating prospects of one more in a succession of avant-gardes to undo precedent and convention, as Gehry would have us believe?[2] Truth may reside in both camps, but how to enable the psychic connectivity of the built Gehry without undoing the particularity of craft and the programmatic elements of a useful object so missing in his work?

Looked at differently, that is accepting and contributing to the progression of technology and the learned elements of making both mental and physical without sacrificing the mysteries born of complex human and nature-based events.

Later, following Gehry's lead in dispelling the myths of Modernism, I researched and wrote about the work of Hannes Meyer and detailed why he had been so disparaged by Gropius and Mies. At the time I didn't fully appreciate the deconstruction I was setting loose in the question that would work to undo Mies and the accepted narrative on Meyer. To my surprise, I found in Meyer's writings, built work and influence as director of the Bauhaus an architectural example of Breton's automatism and a reasonable precursor to Alexander's deterministic methodology. In Meyer, I was hoping to find that similar singular atomic building block for design. So much of his work at the Bauhaus and subsequent brigades in Russia seemed though imbued with a persuasive polemic, nonetheless devoid of spirit.[3] However, I've observed in the recently restored ADGB Trade Union School in Bernau the compositional elegance and thoughtful ordering of manufactured elements that to some degree diverge from his rhetorical rejection of conscious design. Similarly, Le Corbusier's provocative juxtaposition of the Delage "Grand-Sport" racing car with the Parthenon in the *Vers Un Architecture* belies the careful compositions of his maison-atelier Ozenfant that is included in the same publication.[4] Curiously, Meyer was deported from Russia because of his formalism ,whereas he was dismissed from the Bauhaus directorship because his work didn't connect with the political and cultural realities of the time. This may have all contributed to his relative obscurity. From this example, and similar to the debate in physics, I have struggled to find operating mechanisms whereby the predictability of the detail and technological progress, as in Meyer and Mies and the simple patterns of use in Alexander, could be translated into a provocative and nuanced compositional whole greater than its parts and initial impulses. That is, a whole that embraced both the complexities of the cultural realm and the elements of chance found in urban conditions yet still one that could still reference meticulously crafted detail enabling the corporeality of experience.

Wheeler's information theory is based upon a computational strategy of yes/no decisions that seems ideally suited to the digital age yet must seem to architects a mere recitation of Mies' well-known refrain "less is more." Indeed, Wheeler invoked Mies to describe the limitations on the whole derived from a preoccupation with the particular. Wheeler preferred the phrase "more is different" in that his theory, though based upon discrete measurements, could lead to greater and potentially unlimited variability in the whole, or the bit being disguised or at least significantly distorted in the whole.[5] The architecture of the last 25 years, the lion's share of my professional career, has, as Mary McLeod observes "lost its faith in social regeneration that the Modern movement had,"[6] and has retreated from the possibility of deterministic sources to that of the simple animated disembodied projections in light that we find today. Though my reference point has typically been the work and words of other architects, coincidentally, Wheeler provides an equitable benchmark for my ideas outside of the prevailing discourses in architecture. Curious that Wheeler would reference Mies van der Rohe in describing

his "It from Bit" theory of physics. As previously mentioned, shortly after Mies's death, I studied with Alfred Caldwell, who was a colleague of Mies's at IIT before relocating to USC. I felt Caldwell had channeled Mies, even adopting his mannerisms of impeccably tailored suits, restrained lifestyle, serious demeanor and, in his case, the constant cigarette in hand as opposed to Mies' cigar. Of all those early influences, Mies seems the most enigmatic to which I find myself returning, through a clouded memory, unable to shake his web of influence. In school his method seemed suffocating, yet as I began practicing in LA and Utah and later teaching, I found myself constantly tripping over traces of him or, as Beatriz Colomina observed,"the more I found myself [inside Mies' work]."[7] I felt the tangible reminders constantly, as my office was located just a block from the office of Craig Ellwood (who was so influenced by Mies) and John Sugden, a friend and teaching colleague who'd studied and worked under Mies. I continue today to help John's widow with the repairs to his Miesian house in the mountains above Salt Lake, with its elegant plug-welded steel joints, zipper-gasketed glazing and original Barcelona chairs.

The Mies' teaching method as interpreted by Caldwell, allowed for the concurrent method of working the whole to the detail and detail to the whole in some elegantly choreographed dance. The assignments required discipline and rigorously executed hand-drawn details using ink on Strathmore boards. You made a mistake, you started over. In reflection now 40 years later, I realize the detail is more readily extrapolated into the whole when the whole is considerably reduced, as in Mies' buildings. Because Mies limited external influences, he was able to elevate the importance of the classical rule of proportion, the refinement of materials and the integrity of the detail. It seemed to me that because he had limited the urban, climate and cultural engagement of his buildings, other elements were allowed to emerge. This is much like a Chuck Close painting and its imposition of the grid as a means of liberating himself from the influence of the existential painterly gestures of Willem de Kooning.[8] Just as in Close's enabling use of the grid, Mies held his buildings back from the street edge in negating contextual references, cladding them in glass-defying weathering and the passage of time, and elevating them from the ground plane to disassociate from nature. In his high-rise buildings, you literally enter the building through the "reveal" or joint between nature and man-made, that negative space between the upper mass of the building and the ground plane. The reveal in the Modernist convention was used to differentiate between disparate conditions, in this case, between the predictability of the material and the variability of nature. Even the materiality of the buildings, like the furniture, was hidden behind the more expressive qualities of chrome, bronze, onyx, book-matched veneers and finely dyed leathers as Kengo Kuma, observed "to show nature as a symbol, this skin can be chosen."[9] It is said that architects project their own scale into buildings as we find the diminutive scale of Wright's buildings a reflection of his 5'8" height.[10] For Mies it was his personality as much as physique, although that has also been much spoken about. He disengaged from family and even lived in the Blackstone Hotel for three years in Chicago before finding an apartment, keeping his treasured Kandinsky and Klee painting under his bed. His daughter, Georgia questioned this indifference and disas-

sociation towards her and her siblings, "What was he hiding from behind his newspaper, behind his drawings?" Though Mies is so identified with Chicago, he never really embraced the architectural community, culture and history of the place.[11] It seems that Mies was actually quite true to character in his reductive acts that allowed other things to emerge more meaningfully both in character and work. Just as austerity allowed his work to dominate his personal life, the reduced influence of the public domain allowed the detail greater significance in his architecture.

The doing of architecture seems to have its own logic that now seems borne up by quantum theory. Mies's idea of atomization may have mimicked Einstein's desire for certainty and thus became the essence for Modernist utopian thinking. The idea of the importance of the particular to design may have its origins in the Greek refinements, Roman miniaturization and more succinctly in the Islamic aesthetic theory of atomization. Can this long history and reoccurring idea of the centrality of the detail as a potential determinant for design have relevance today? The challenge in reflection is the unavoidable historical perspective of Derrida, that one cannot escape that which renders any empirical attempt at absolutes utterly impossible. [12] To some degree Mies may have foreshadowed the nihilism that is attributable to Derrida in his refusal to engage. Yet in architecture the promise of early Modernism and its fealty to the empirical , its resistance to authorship in order to empower utility and it's hope to improve the general welfare still seems plausible. As Einstein said, "God is subtle but he is not malicious."[13]

Our work has endeavored to provide a platform for engagement that transcends in an assertive way the nearsighted science of sustainable technologies on the one hand and the rhetoric of infinitely adaptable surface treatments on the other. Unlike the post-structuralist critique that each act of will invariably is accomplished at the expense of another rendering all acts irreconcilable and thus equivalent, I propose an architecture based upon simple acts of observation and measurement or what Niels Bohr calls registration that can be accumulated while allowing adjustment and assemblage in a cloud of probability where certainty and uncertainty may coexist. The response to a certain instance or instrumentality derived from simple observation does not necessarily preclude other options and may invite serendipity. This is not an architecture of absolutes yet does not close out it's possibility and thus noticeably veers from the historical utopian origins of Modernism and its provocations.

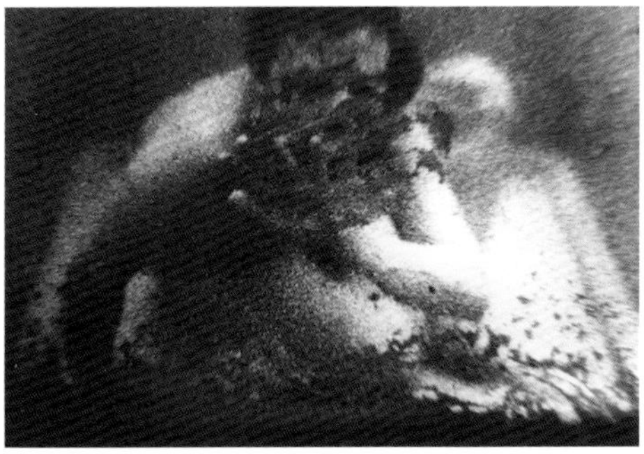

In architecture, there currently is little talk of truth , beauty or absolutes of any kind. Can this process that accepts the credibility of measurable outcomes rescue the possibility of absolutes if only at some primitive level? I think architecture can and should afford more nuanced meaning than mere reduction to the authenticity of the architects gesture or churlish infatuation with one's body as in Mona Hatoum's work. Yet as long as we reside in bodies it is the point of mediation with the material world. Juhani Pallasma observes in a similar perspective, "architecture cannot however become an instrument of mere functionality, bodily comfort and sensory pleasure without losing its existentially mediating task."[14] Probably at the detriment of representing our work in a cohesive way, it has endeavored to resist the formulaic as well as figurative impulses. Thus, each project is "different," yet I hope there is a thread of continuity that comes with the cloud of probability derived from a dependence upon measurables. I would characterize our work as one of abduction rather than induction. That is, the body of work is based upon the reconciliation of myriad small issues of certifiable origins. The grouping or assemblage of these doodads or proofs works to undo the idea just as the idea can't hope to merely reflect the particular. Each project, in being grounded in the programmatic and situational, resists the globalization found in the replicability of mere idea-based designs. However, the method itself is certainly not place-bound.

An inductive approach is one based upon a hypothesis in search of program resulting in content that is transported in an alienated vessel. Indeed, the inductive or preconceived models speak of the English poet, John Keats' notion of the sublimely creative act as some "Dionysian frenzy." What Romanticism initiated as epiphanic rapture or a foil to the historical becomes in our own time an epistemic rupture.[15] More specifically, the inadvertent gesture is now masquerading as some refusal to act that has become the common currency in both practice and the academy. Ironically, the inductive approach invites the very commercialization or reification that gesture-based designs intended to negate. The inductive work invariably becomes the "bloody Doric column" barely concealing itinerant political forces.

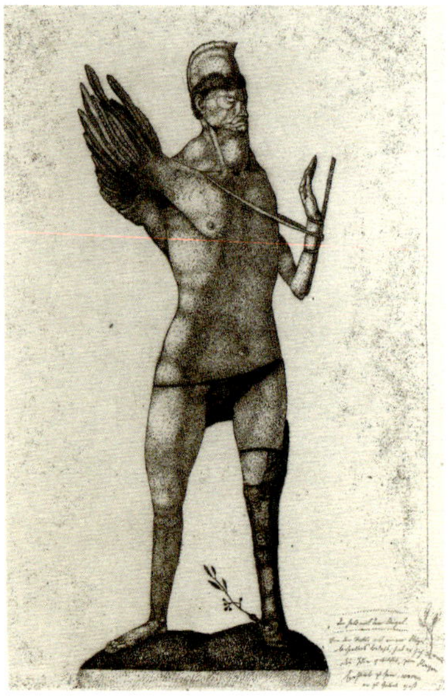

Paul De Man observed in reading Confessions, Rousseau's preoccupation between useless facts and pure *fiction* that experience always exists simultaneously as both fictional discourse and empirical event [with the impossibility] to decide which "one is the right one."[16] An architectural equivalent would be a demonstrable proof that contains both a compositional quality of proportional determinants of beauty as well as measurements found in the material. A concession to relativism is a denial of architecture's redemptive capacity and extinguishes any opportunity for the regeneration found in tropes. As ecosystems are facing collapse, the cultural implications for sustainable technologies are as important as ever. Carlos Ginzburg has an apt characterization "...sources are neither open windows [to truth] as positivists would argue or fences obstructing truth as the relativists argue but [are] distorting mirrors...."[17]

During the formative years of 20th-century Modernism, Bertolt Brecht suggested that "the bad old things have protected us from the bad new things...."[18] In light of Derrida and the post-structuralists, the bad old things have been undone and cannot provide a reliable source nor continuing threat. So what is a reliable point of intervention or entry into the cultural realm that avoids the associated traps of technology found in Corbu's Delage racing car? We are in a period in which the architectural world has lost its bearing and entered some state of lost cognition or historical amnesia. Just as a patient suffering brain injury, we must recreate our reality to learn to walk and to learn to build with confidence again. Those of us who do architecture and who do build, we understand the certain undeniability of the natural world: wood has a specific grain, steel has certain thermal characteristics and both subject and material can and do matter.

I am willing to acknowledge that the faceted details of assemblage can contribute to Wheeler's cloud of probability as it expands by accident as much as purpose into a complex and varied whole. This doesn't preclude a simple point of origin, the shadow of which may be perceived in the whole. I am willing to believe that sources may exist and that each, though distorted, may be reflected in the "it to bit" just as in the "bit to it". The appropriate positioning of architecture is a suspension of absolutes, utopias and naïve positivism as much as an equal suspicion of form derived from the purely intuitive or the existential gesture of the author as though it were some authentic act worthy of celebration. This is an architecture calibrated somewhere between the extremes of the feel-good determinism of New Urbanism or the vacuous formalism of parametricity. The purely intuitive and utopian premise is extinguished in favor of a series of accumulated proofs and clues that merely imply a plausible projection into the complexities and accidents of the urban/cultural realm. If reflected impressions and obdurate registration in the fractures found in Duchamp's *The Large Glass* provide a reliable paradigm for engagement, then the resultant artifact thus deflecting preconception will imply both the possibilities in an open-ended proposition, a proposition for architecture.

Notes:

1. John Archibald Wheeler with Kenneth Ford, Geons, *Black Holes and Quantum Foam* (New York: W.W. Norton and Company, 1998) p.339-342.
2. Renato Poggioli, *The Theory of the Avant-Garde* (Cambridge, MA: The Belknap Press of Harvard University, 1968), p.192.
3. Prescott Muir, "Automatic Determinism or the Devil in Mr. Meyer," *On Architecture, the City, and Technology,* ed. Marc Angelil (New York: Butterworth Architectural Press, 1990), p.58.
4. Le Corbusier, *Vers Un Architecture* (New York: Praeger Publishers,1960), p.125.
5. Wheeler, p.340-341.
6. Mary McLeod, "Architecture and Politics in the Reagan Era: From Postmodernism to Deconstructivism," *Assemblage 8*, ed. Michael Hays (Cambridge, MA: MIT Press, 1989), p. 45.
7. Beatriz Colomina, "Mies Not," *The Presence of Mies*, ed. Detlef Mertins (New York: Princeton Architectural Press, 1994), p.194.
8. Mira Locher, *Traditional Japanese Architecture*, (Tokyo: Tuttle Publishing, 2010), p. 8.
9. Charlie Rose, video interview with Chuck Close, 13 Mar. 2003.
10. Changing Parts, Mona Hatoum, 1984 courtesy of White Cube Art, LLP
10. Edgar Tafel, *Years with Frank Lloyd Wright* (New York: Dover Press, 1979), p. 20.
11. Franz Schulze, Mies van der Rohe, *A Critical Biography* (Chicago: The University of Chicago Press, 1985), p. 218.
12. *Derrida*, dir. Kirby Dick and Amy Ziering Kofman, Jane Doe Films, 2002.
13. Wheeler, p. 25.
14. Juhani Pallasmaa, *The Eyes of the Skin* (Chichester, England: John Wiley & Sons, 2005), p. 62.
15. Ihab Hassan, *The Dismemberment of Orpheus* (Madison, WI: The University of Wisconsin Press, Ltd., 1982), p. 7; note #11, p. 303.
16. Paul De Man, *Allegories of Reading* (New Haven, CT: Yale University Press, 1979), p. 293 .
17. Carlo Ginzburg, *History, Rhetoric, and Proof* (Hanover, NH: Brandeis University Press, 1999), p. 25.
18. Carlo Ginzburg, *The Judge and the Historian* (New York: Verso, 1999), p.16.

Images:

1. *Portrait of Niels Bohr and Albert Einstein* by Paul Ehrenfest, 1925
2. Prescott Muir School Project at USC, 1971
3. *Automatic Drawing,* Andre Masson, 1924
4. ADGB Trade Union Building, Bernau, Hannes Meyer, 1930
5. *Vers Une Architecture*, Le Corbusier
6. *Fractal Mathematics With Business Cards,* Redux Pictures
7. *Portrait of Alfred Caldwell and Mies van der Rohe*, Domer @ Johns Hopkins University
8. *Maggie,* Chuck Close, 1996 courtesy Pace Gallery
9. *Mies in Apartment with Klee*, Getty Images
10. *The Hero With the Wing,* Paul Klee, 1904
11. *The Bride Stripped Bare by her Bachelors Even or Large Glass,* Marcel Duchamp, 1915-1923

ROSE WAGNER PERFORMING ARTS CENTER

Salt Lake City, Utah

Salt Lake supports fledgling resident arts companies and their desire to incubate new works in a risk-free environment. The Wagner Center provides a center for experimentation, idea development and presentation. Walls are intended to welcome the merging of the memory of construction and performers alike as the spaces are marked and registered for both fabrication and artistic interpretation. Preconceptions are challenged by the juxtaposition of refined material like silver leaf with that of plywood, ground-faced concrete block and marble façade with galvanized steel cornice. Passersby are celebrated as performers in a reflection on the mirror-finished stone face that is canted to bring greater focus to the sidewalk as a stage.

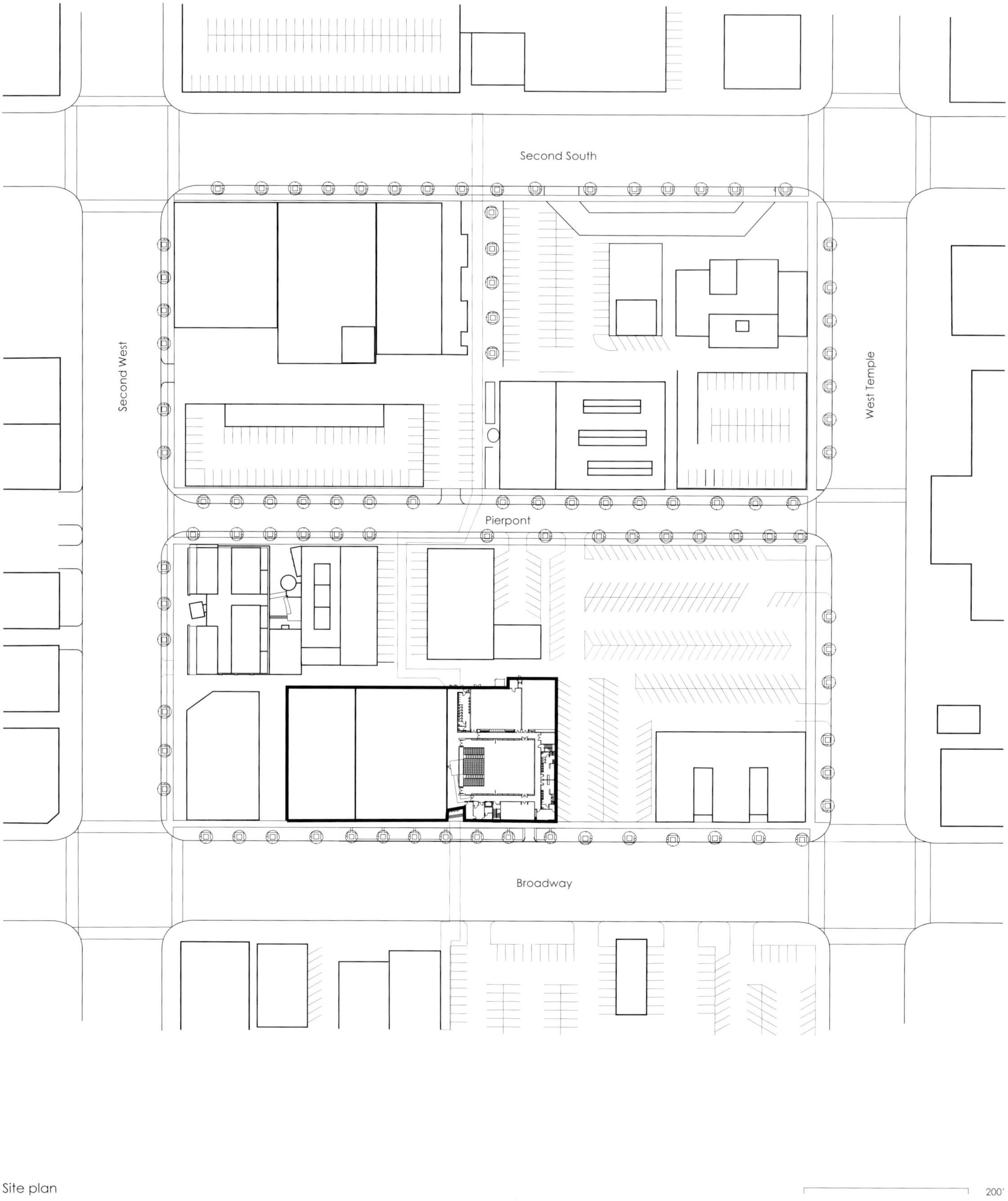
Second South
Second West
West Temple
Pierpont
Broadway
200'

Site plan

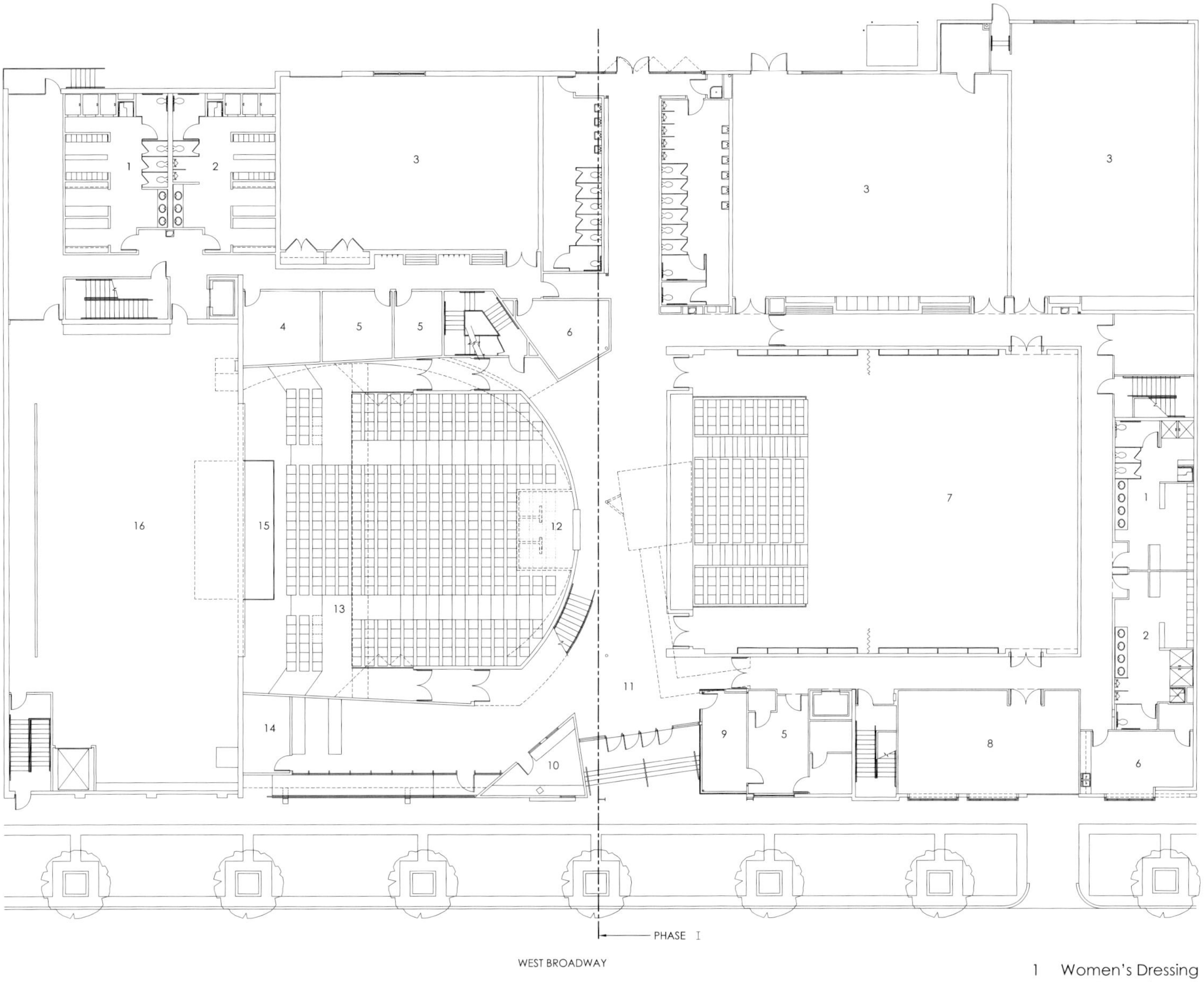

1 Women's Dressing
2 Men's Dressing
3 Studio
4 Manager
5 Office
6 Green Room
7 Black-Box Theater
8 Staging
9 Gift Shop
10 Ticket Booth
11 Lobby
12 Coat Room
13 500-Seat Theater
14 Concessions
15 Orchestra Pit
16 Stage

Main floor plan

32'

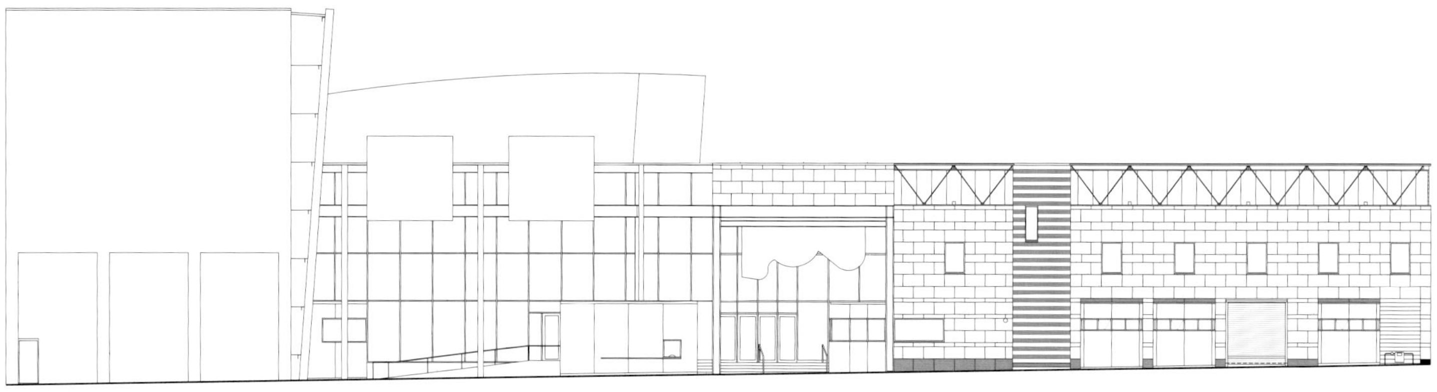

South elevation

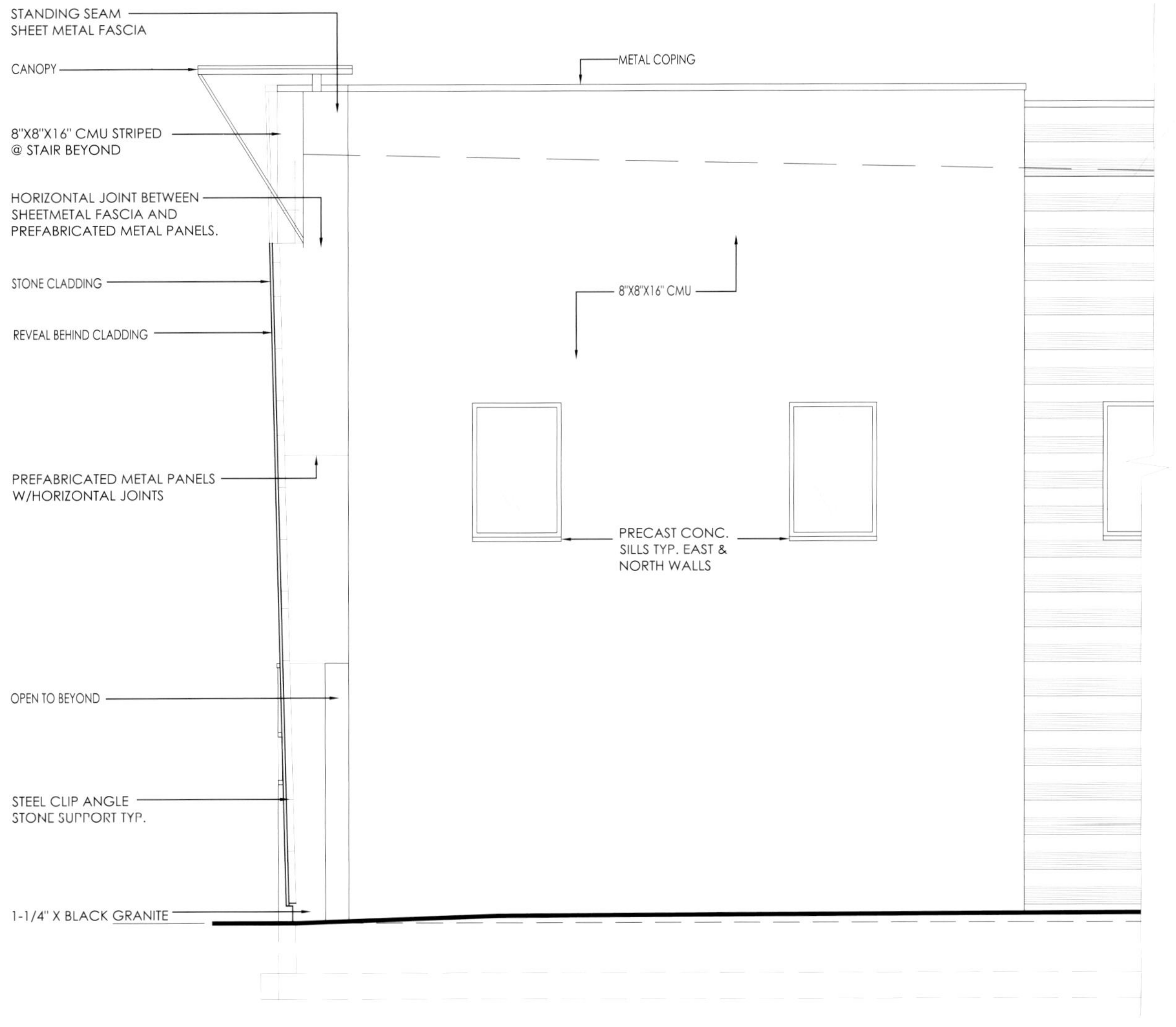

Partial east elevation

INTERMODAL HUB

Salt Lake City, Utah

Salt Lake, known as the crossroads of the West, has always been a railroad town, with the original development of Salt Lake and Ogden growing off their great railroad terminals in a succession of hotels and commerce. Not even the Mormon Temple violates the grid as do these depots. Contemporary transportation hubs are little more than platforms for waiting yet contain the DNA of these grand portals to the city. The design to this competition was to recapture several existing produce-loading sheds as part of two armatures that embrace Second South Street, which is the main link connecting the eastern and western parts of the city. In a simple series of gestures using primarily the utilitarian alignment of tracks, bus bays and an exceptionally large canopy for the small terminal building, the design provides an open embrace to the city.

Main floor plan

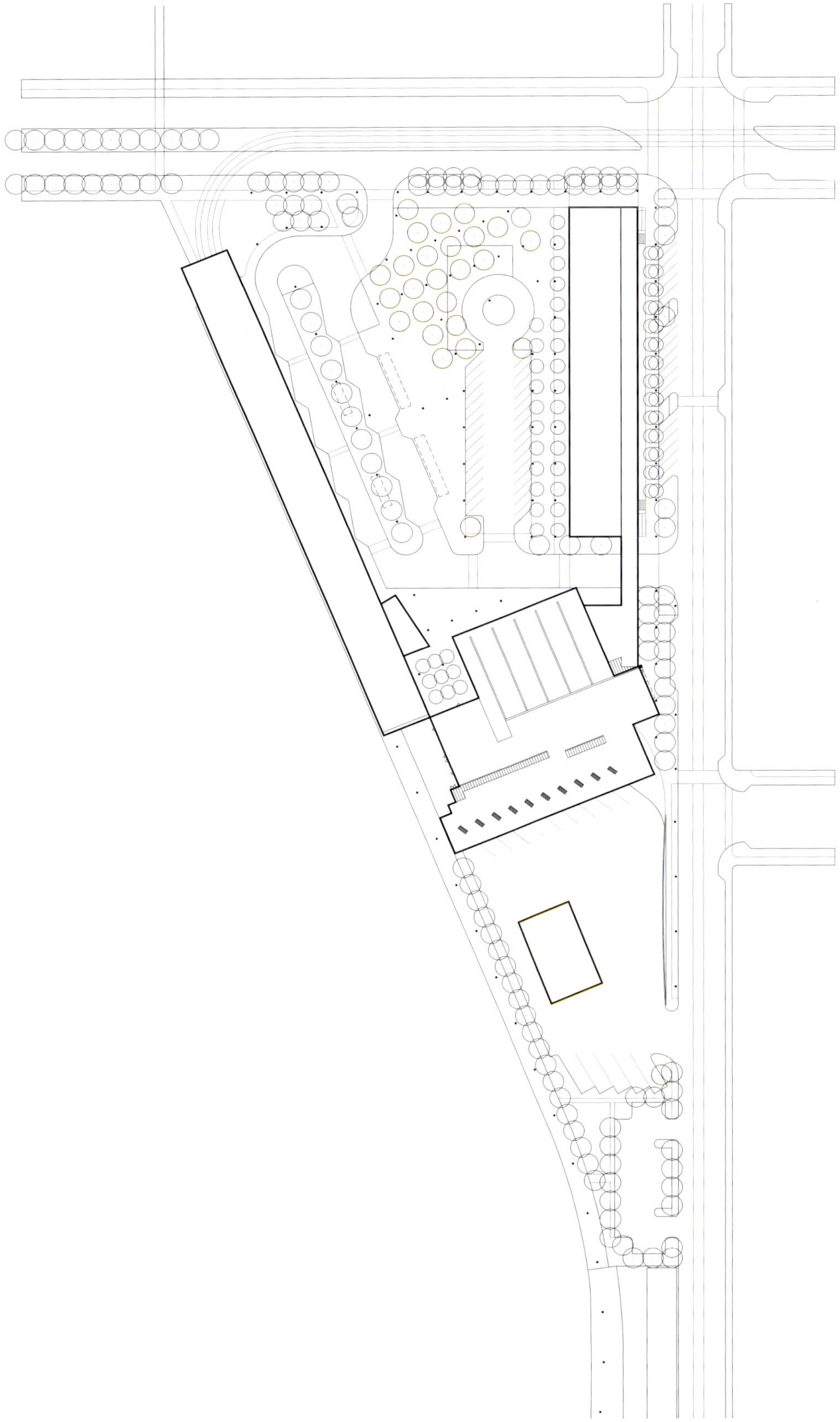

Site plan

120'

BRIDGE MIXED-USE PROJECT

Salt Lake City, Utah

Phase 1

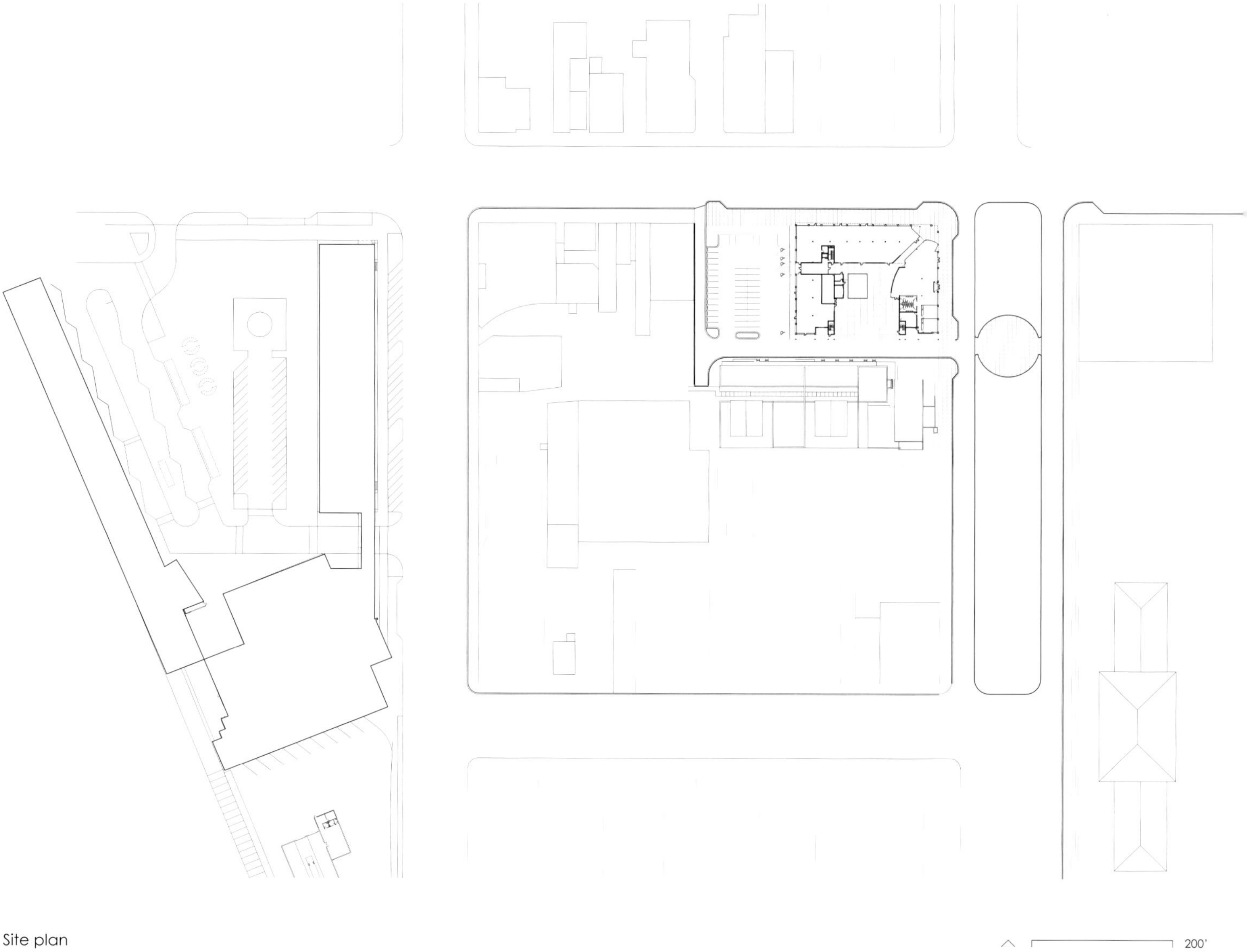

Site plan

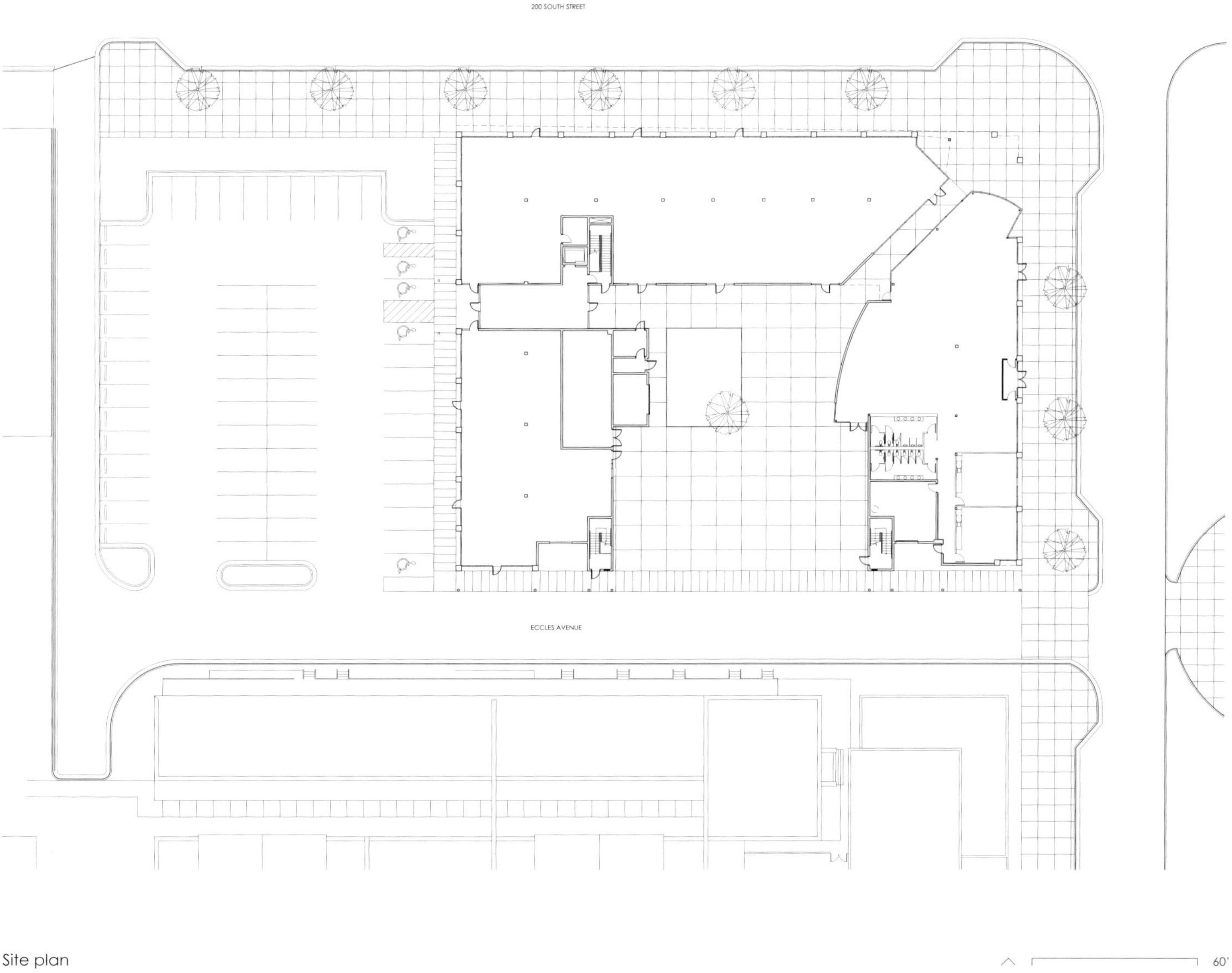

Site plan

The west side neighborhoods in Salt Lake are some of the most diverse in the United States with over 20 languages spoken in the schools. The Bridge Affordable and Mixed-Use Housing project was one of the first to be built in the old railyard redevelopment area of the city. The housing element surrounds a south-facing interior courtyard that gathers the winter sun like Anasazi Cliff dwellings and provides a community precinct augmented by the sun. The skin of the building is an aggressive wrapper of deep-ribbed steel siding that is discretely stripped away to reveal the interior courtyard and recessed balconies clad in taut red siding. This is a HUD affordable housing project where small amenities like 9-foot ceilings and shelves at entries to set groceries on are major achievements. The commercial base level includes a community gallery, home for Tree Utah, a community radio station and Spyhop, which is a nonprofit independent film company. The master plan included a Buddhist temple and dedicated area in the street for its annual Oban Festival.

South elevation

East elevation

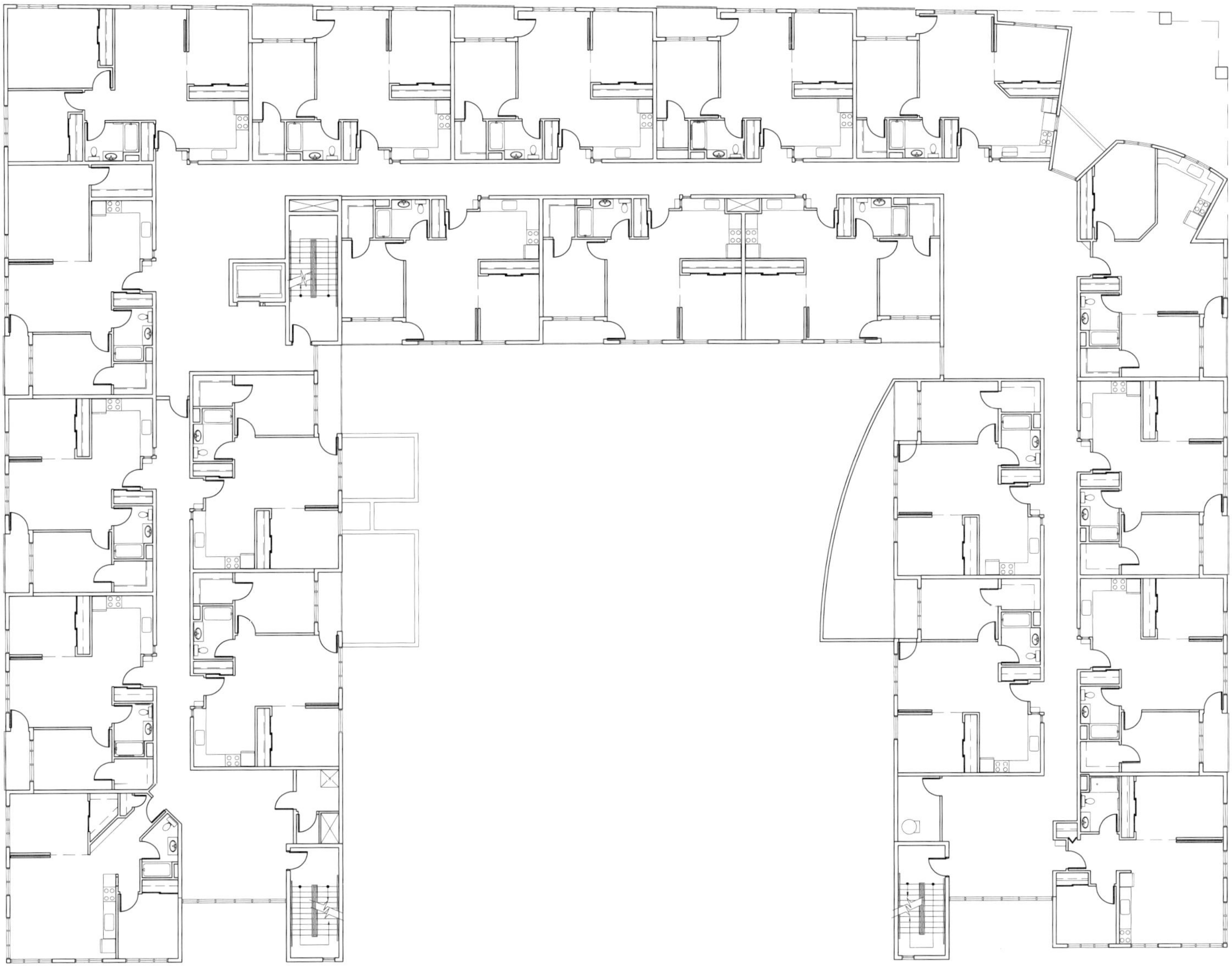

Second floor plan

32'

SALT LAKE CITY ART CENTER
Salt Lake City, Utah

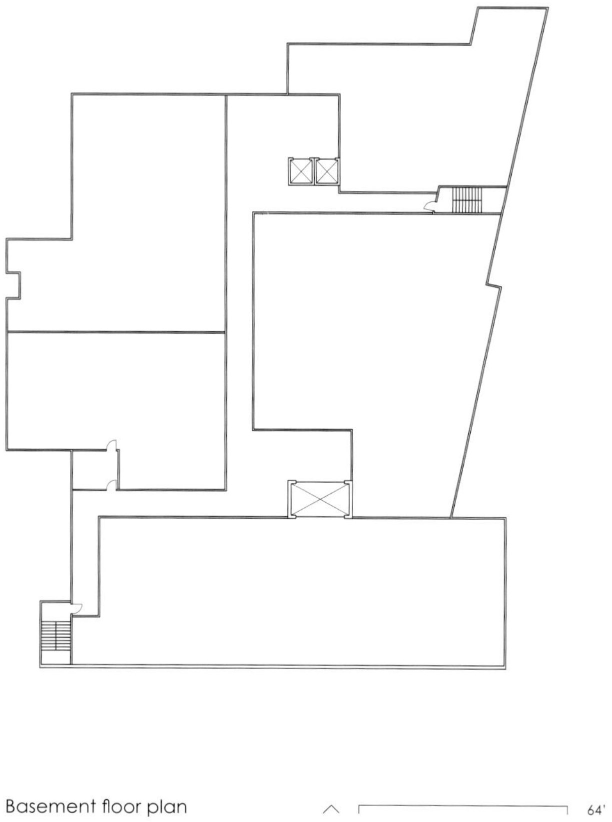

Basement floor plan

The New Art Building will complete the north edge of Salt Lake's Gallivan Plaza. It is the center stage for outdoor events and concerts. The Art Center will have a walking connection to the new 2,500-seat theater on Main Street. It is Utah's premier exhibition space for modern art. The program will include grand gallery space, two exhibit galleries, one gallery dedicated to traveling exhibits, administrative offices, storage, framing, shipping and receiving, café, outdoor seating and an outdoor sculpture plaza that engages the city.

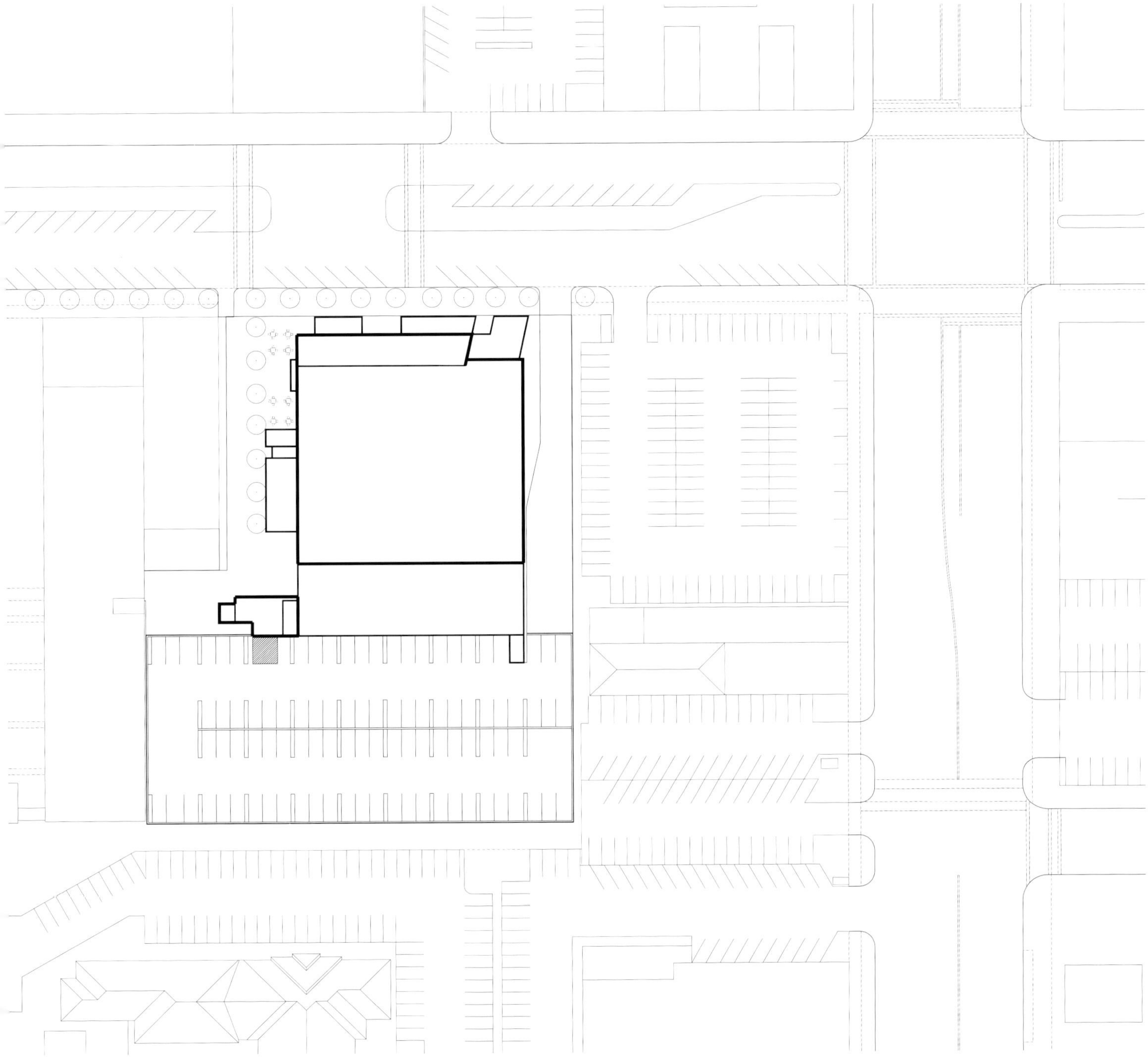

Site plan

128'

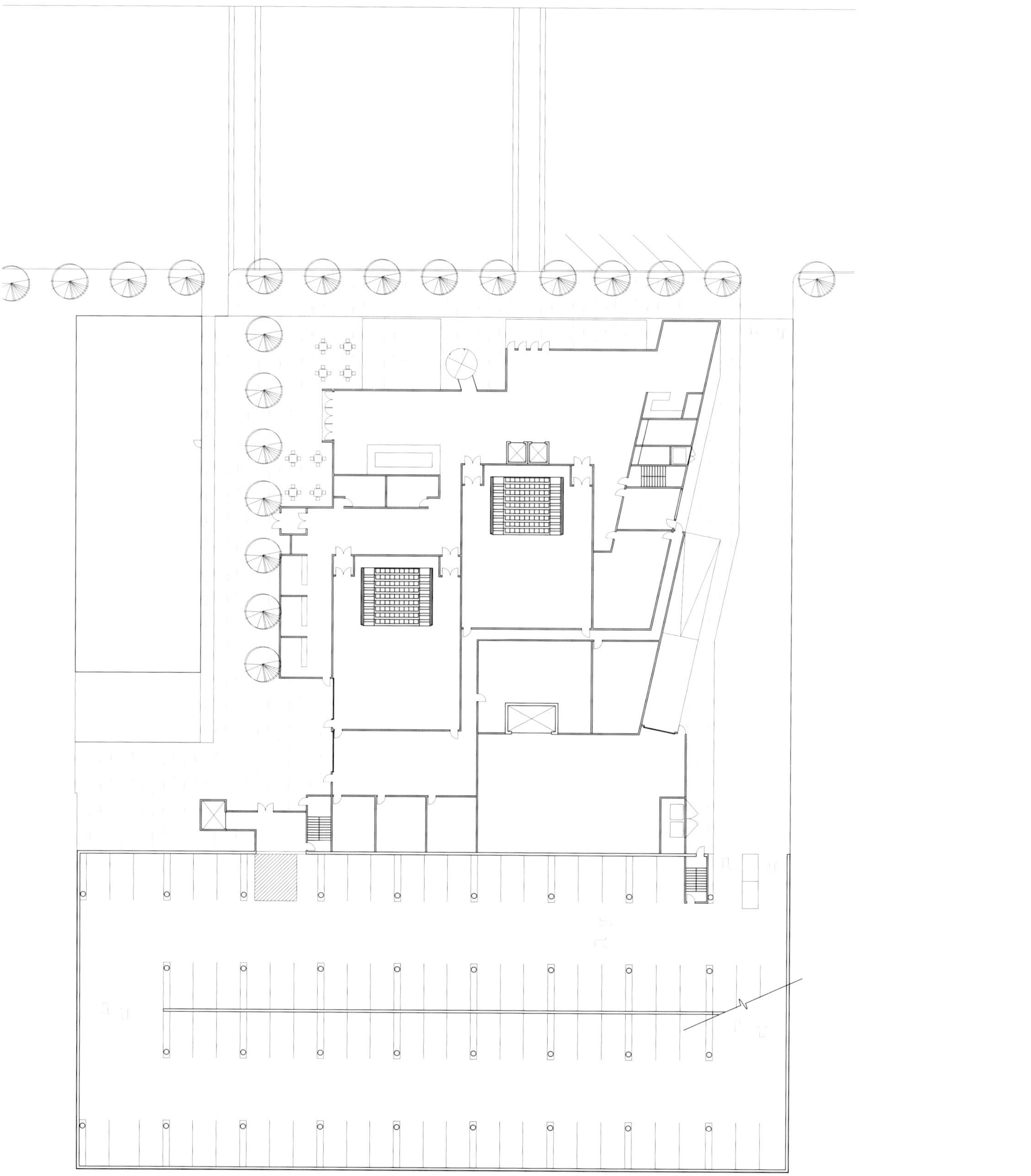

Main floor plan

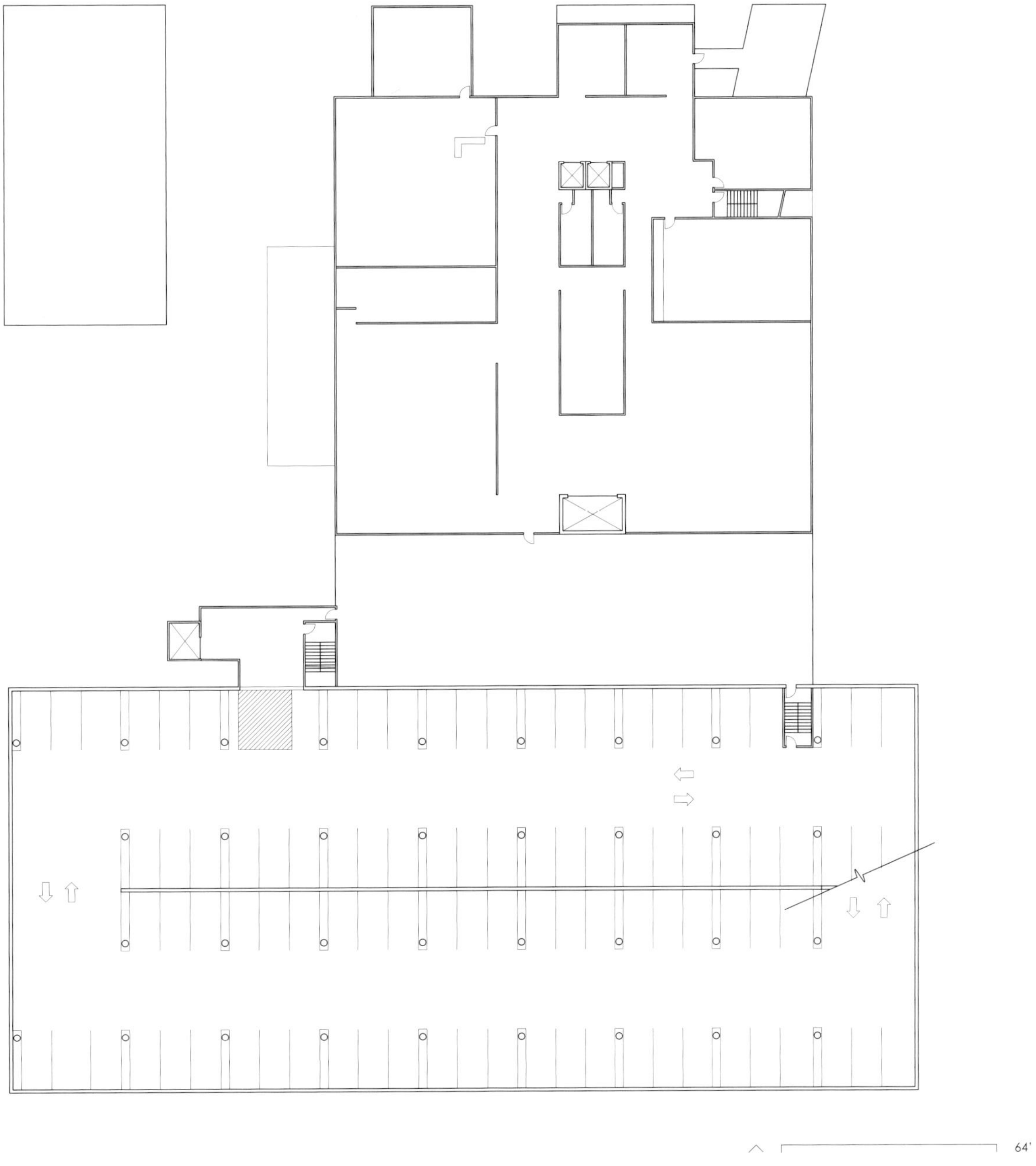

Second floor plan

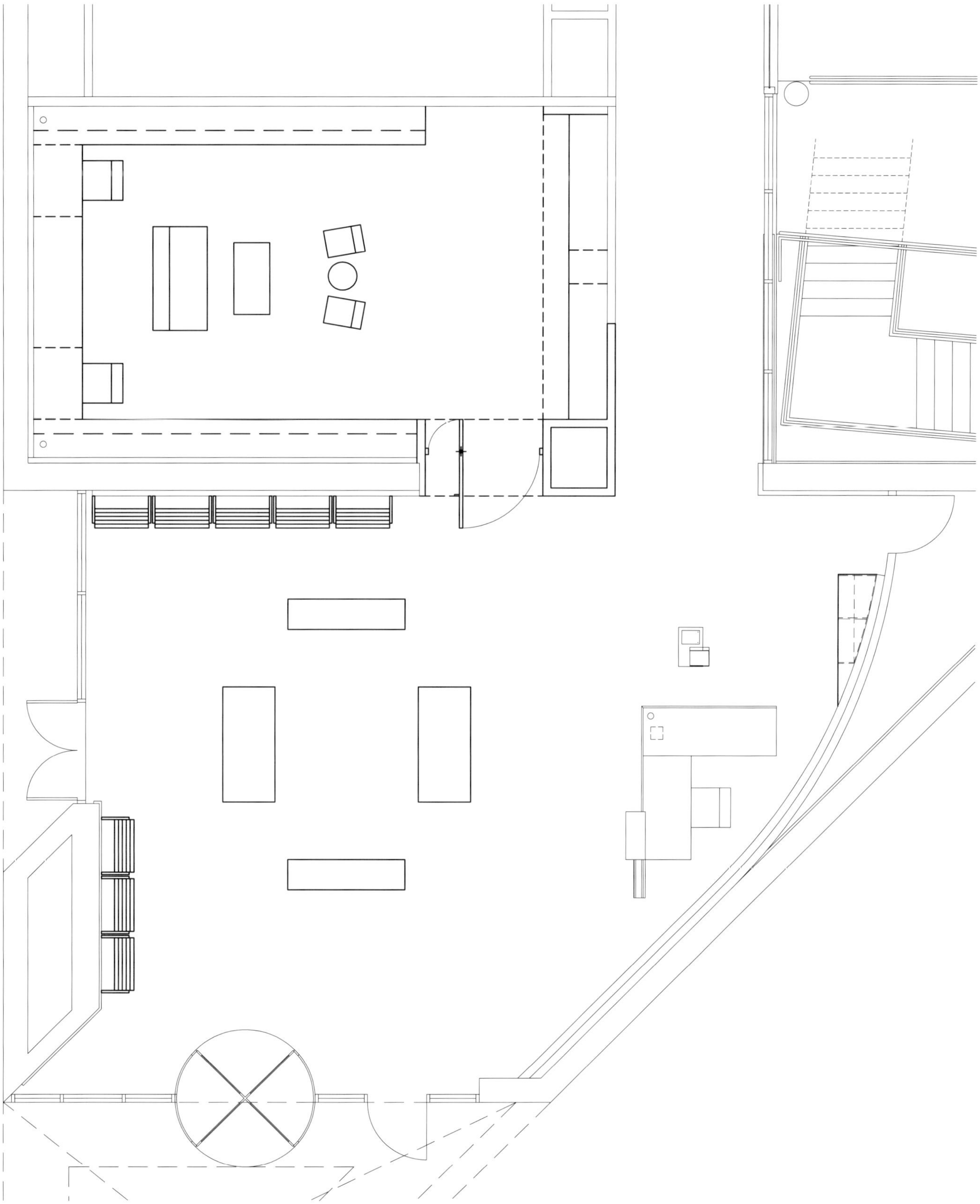

Main floor plan

8'

Prescott Muir and the office have been involved with the Salt Lake Art Center for over 30 years, providing technical support to their exhibits and design for their gift shop, lobby and education gallery. In 2008 the Center looked to expand to an emerging cultural district that Prescott had master-planned for the City. The plan included the location of a future Broadway Theater and film institute. The master plan envisioned a center that includes artist housing as a profit center and complimentary use.

The juxtaposition of a museum and housing combines a series of open and closed propositions between the need to be inviting on the public face to make the art seem more accessible and closed to provide security for the collection at the non-public areas and to the housing entry. The galleries are closed as well, in that they require controlled light to conserve the collection and enhance the aura of the objects displayed. The building once again opens up in the private residences above the street as they face the views to Gallivan Plaza and the mountains beyond. The proposed design is choreography between open and closed forms.

ETHEL WATTIS KIMBALL
DEPARTMENT OF VISUAL ARTS

Weber State University

Ogden, Utah

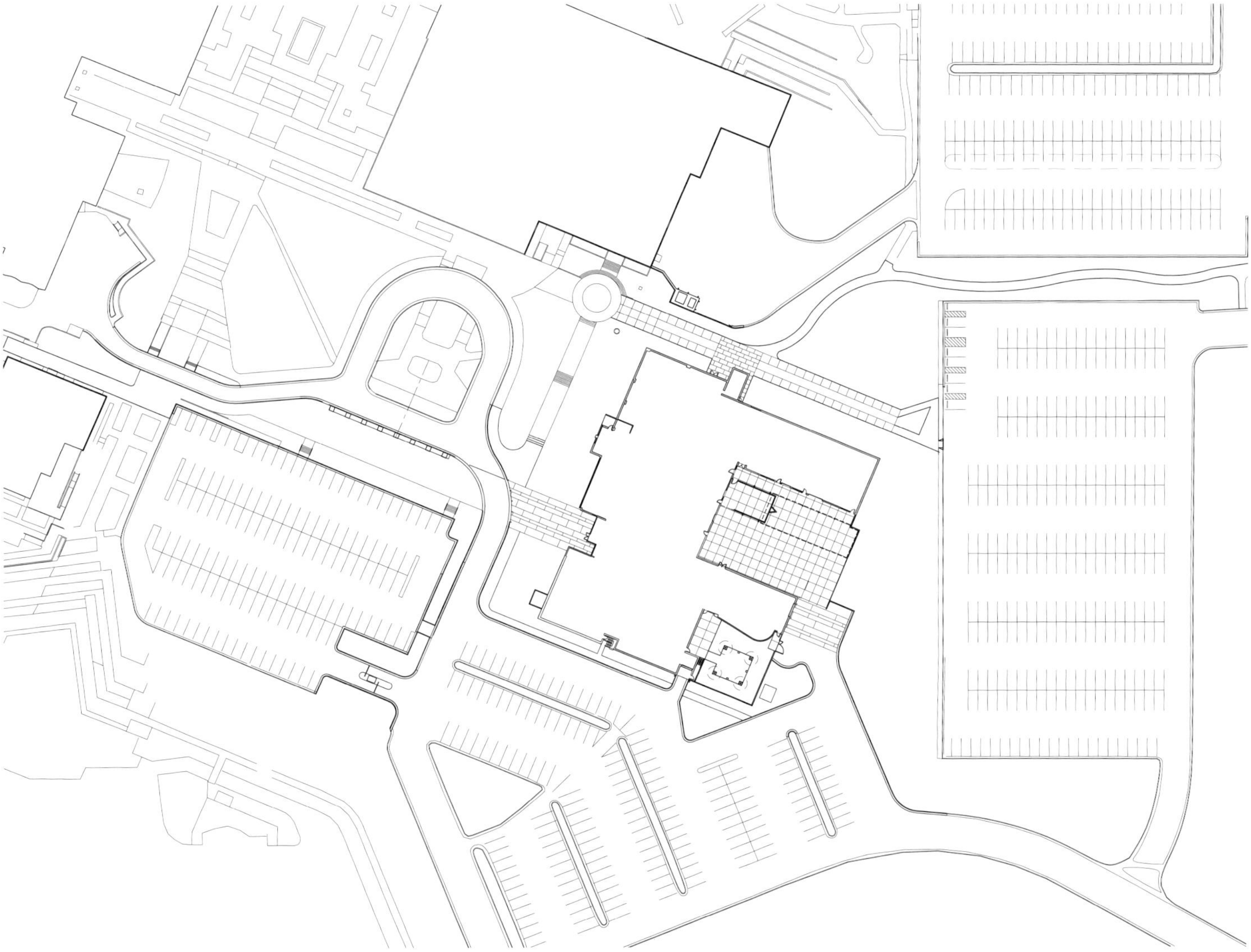

Site plan

In a singular building, the Kimball Center accommodates the future development of a central campus quadrangle as well as internally anticipates the transition from analog-based technique to digitally-premised idea generation. Within the normative natural lit studios scaled to a body-centric engagement with materials, technique and display resides the opportunity to undo the normative in a future dominated by digital curriculum that is disembodied from location and scale. Just as in a program that anticipates its own undoing, the structural integrity of the building is subverted by folding conventional steel decking to invite natural light into the gallery envelope, where structural integrity becomes light that marks the temporal passage of time.

ETHEL
KIM
WATTIS

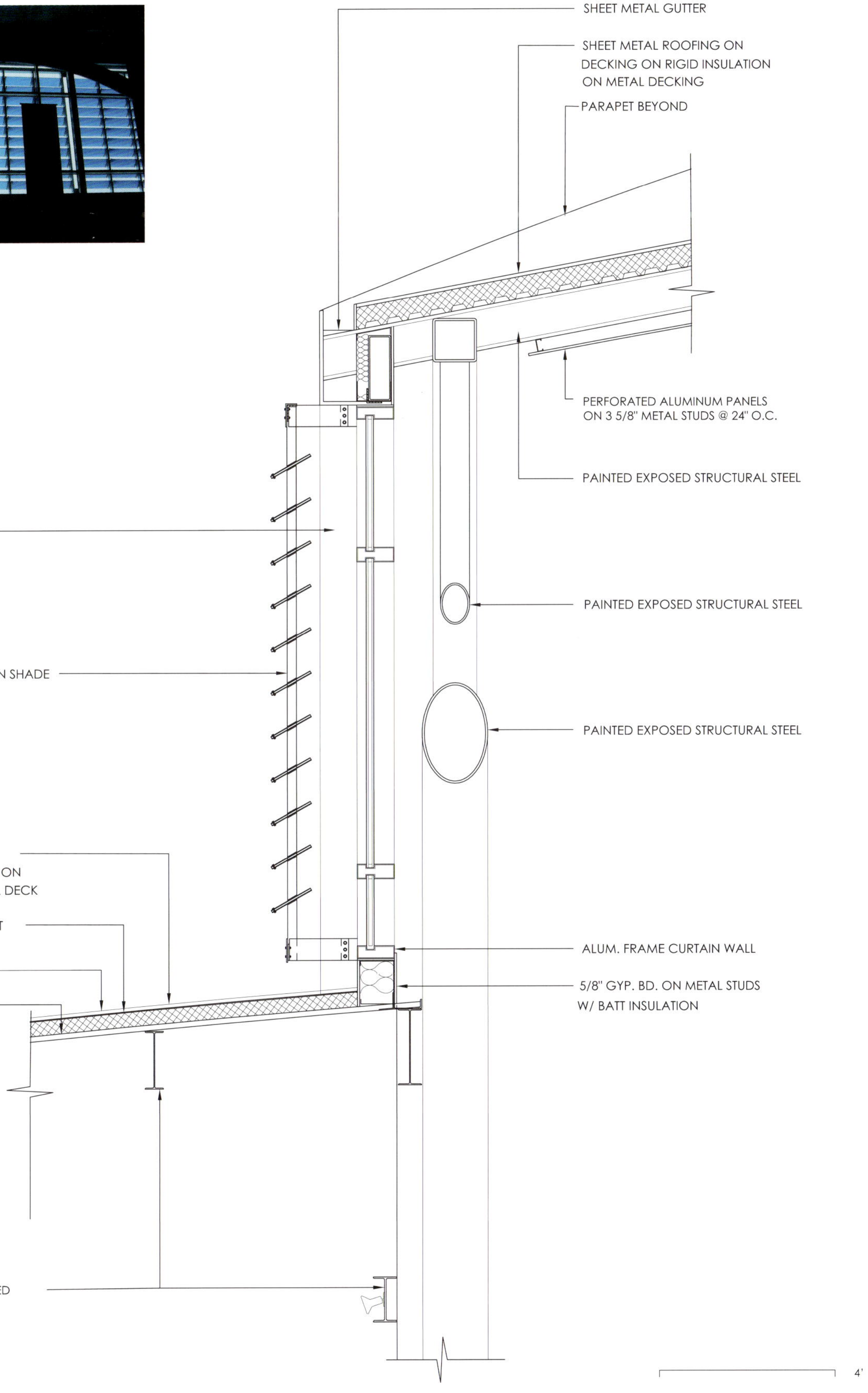

Louver details

154

ETHEL WATTIS KIMBALL
VISUAL ARTS
CENTER

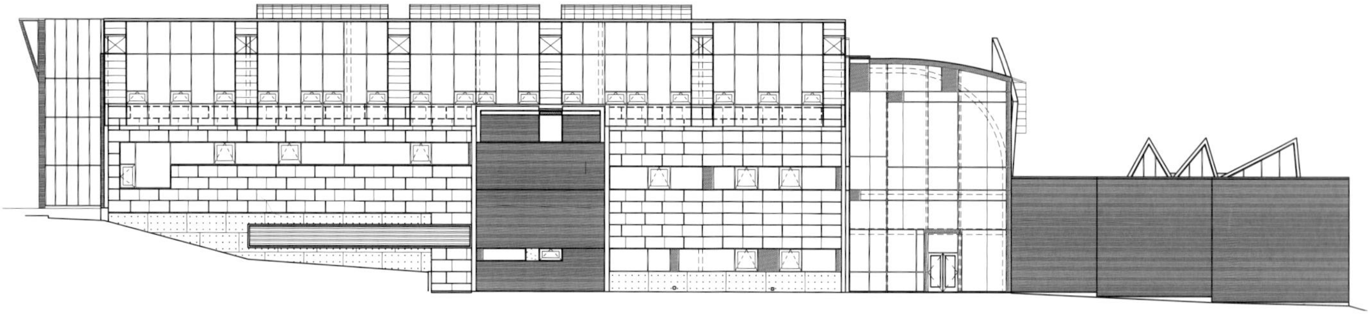

North elevation

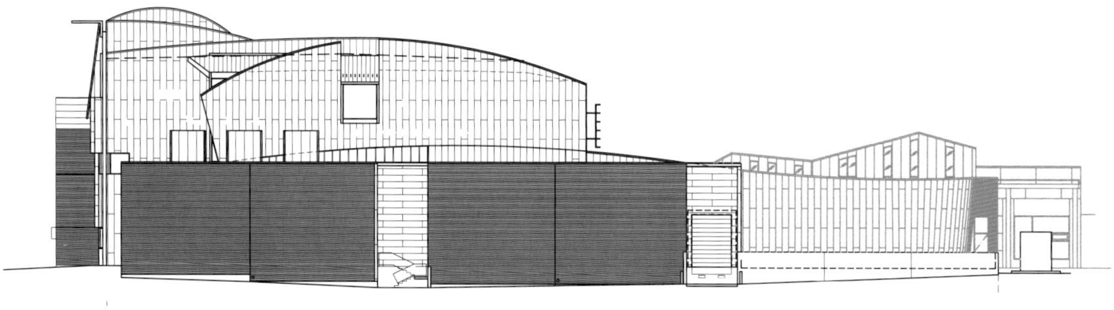

West elevation

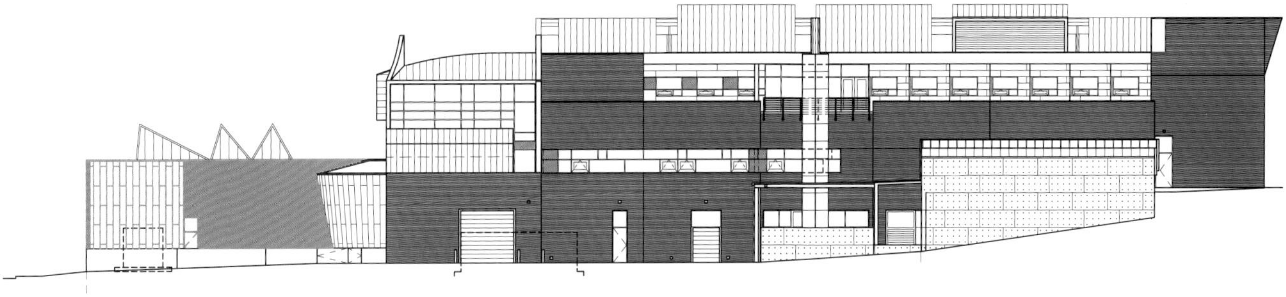

South elevation

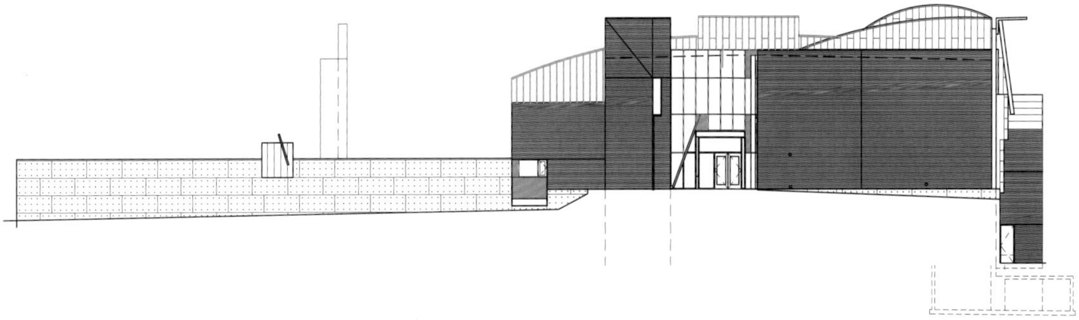

East elevation

64'

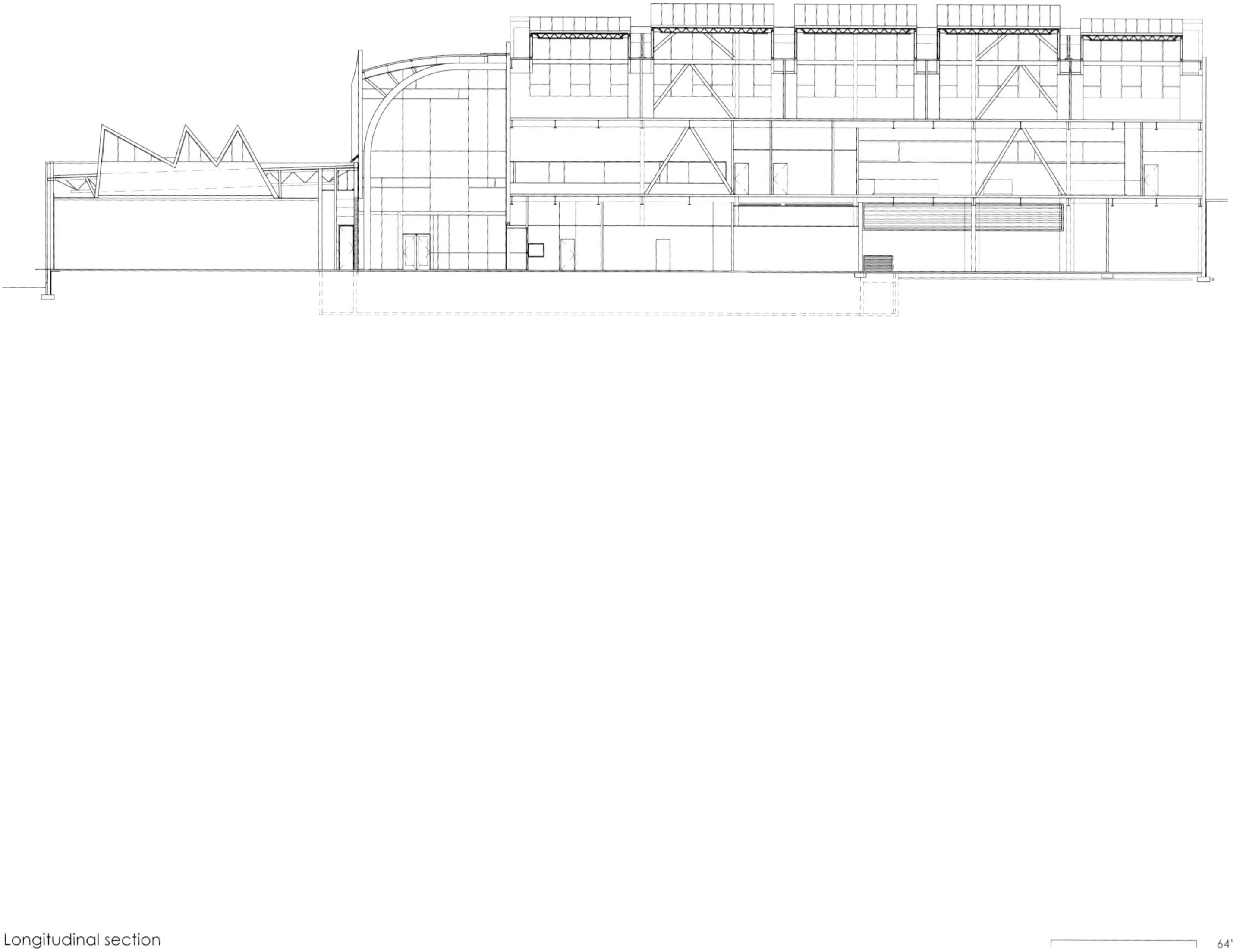

Longitudinal section

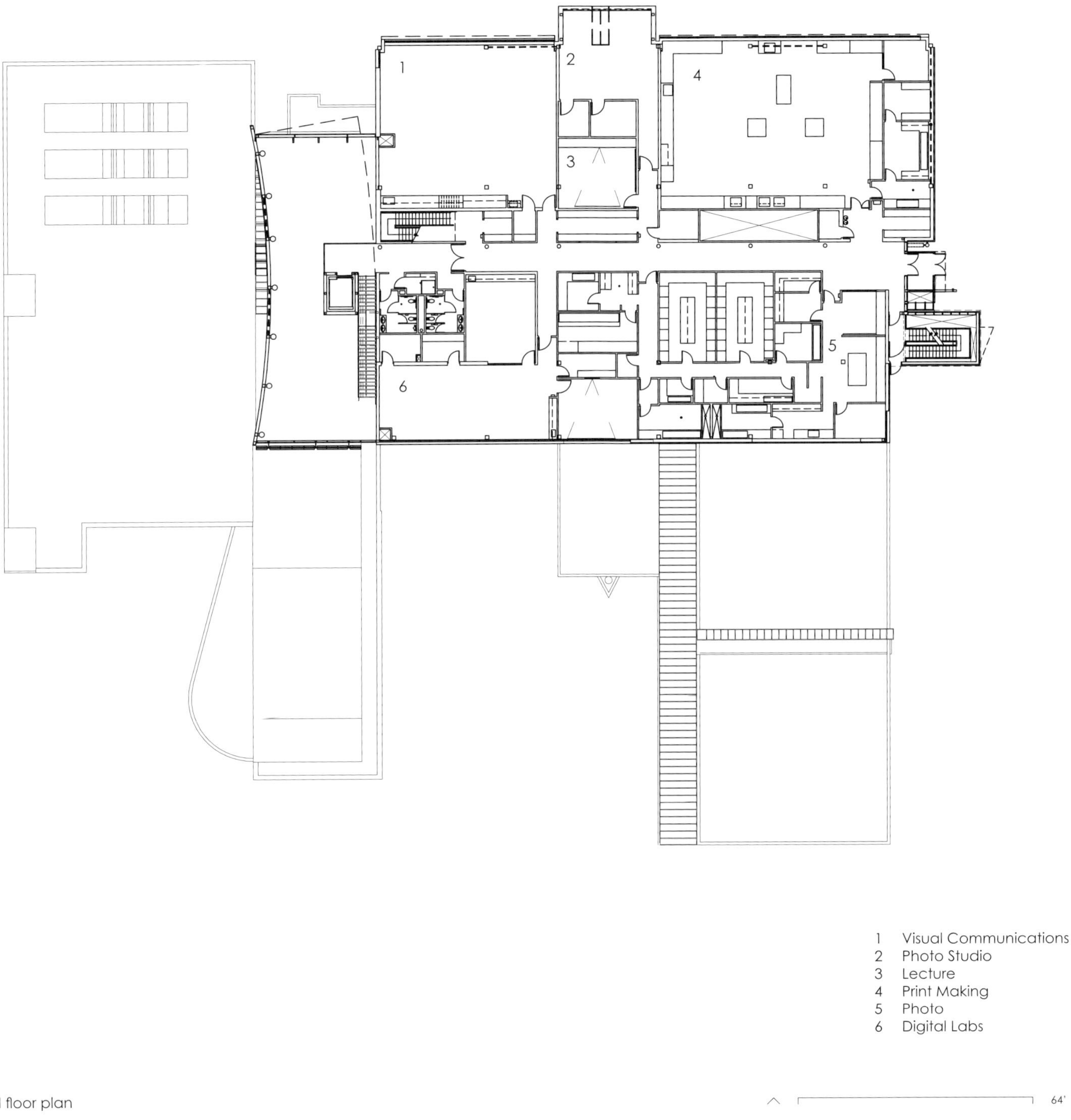

1 Visual Communications
2 Photo Studio
3 Lecture
4 Print Making
5 Photo
6 Digital Labs

Second floor plan

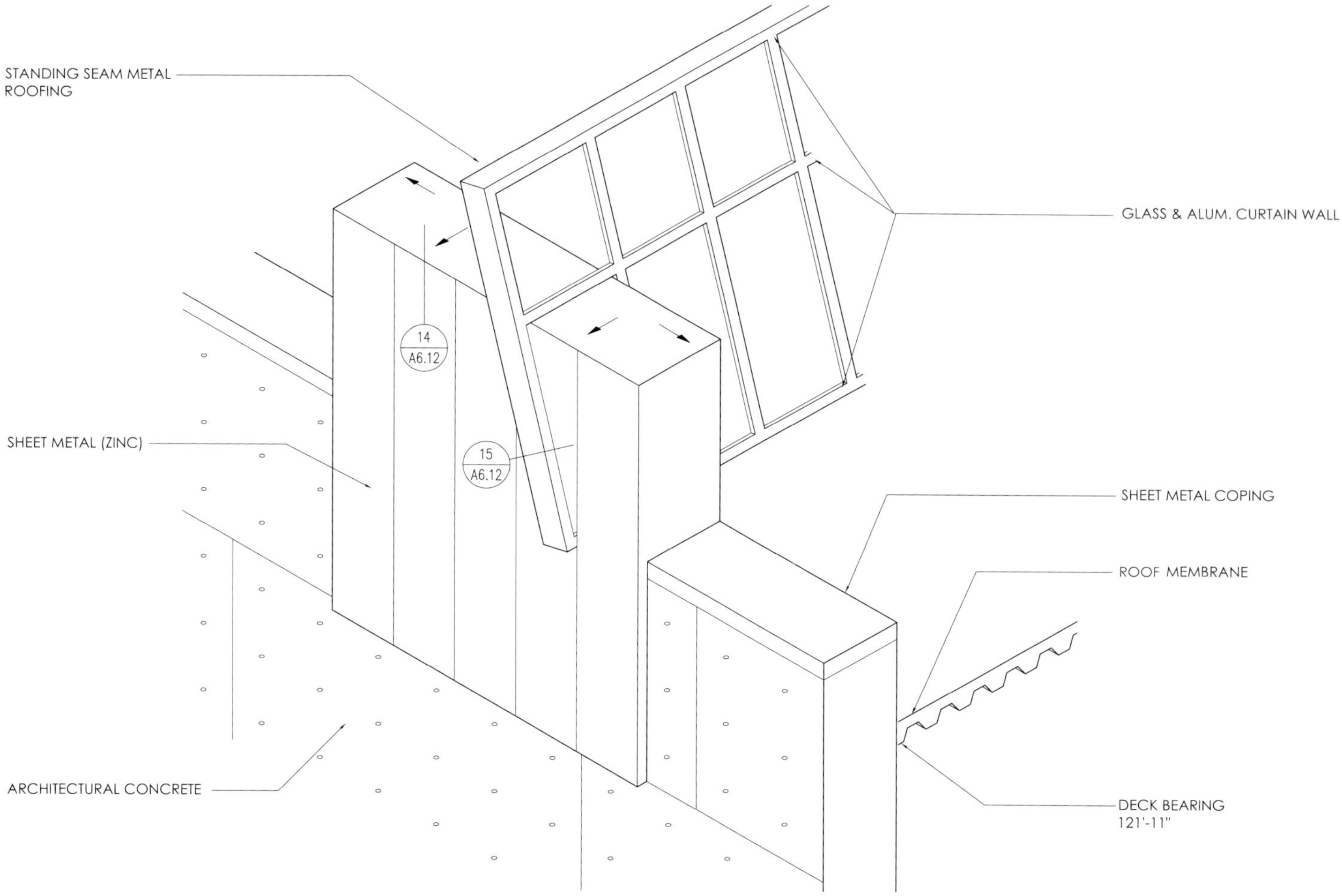

Skylight details

MARY ELIZABE

VISUAL ARTS CENTER
GRAND OPENING CELEBRATION MAY 23-24, 2002
SPONSORED BY WELLS FARGO BANK
WILLIAM RICE KIMBALL
BROWNING
BARBARA KIMBALL
ECCLES

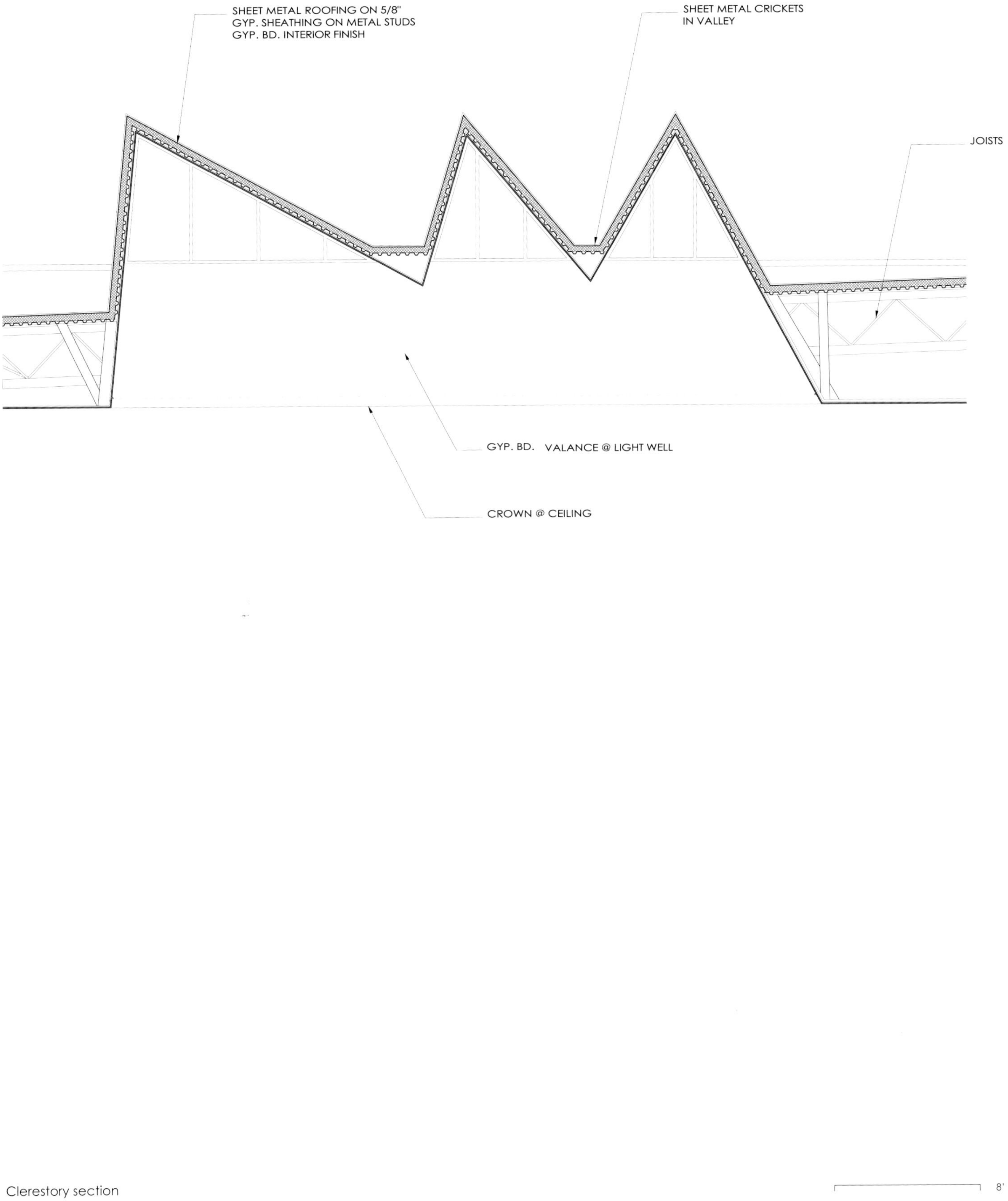

Clerestory section

ETH

BLOX
Salt Lake City, Utah

What is the narrative that brings together numerous found objects, an existing printing house and grain silo? These are tropes shorn of original meaning and repurposed as the factory becomes the studio and the silo a staircase. The silo is constructed as though a palimpsest of primitive Anasazi patterns emerged from the ground to become a shaft of light. The building is about a reduction to its bare essence of in-situ-poured concrete and windows that embrace the body. Details of new interventions are merely used to showcase artifacts such as the stair, which is simply inserted in the silo without mechanical connection. Subject can matter.

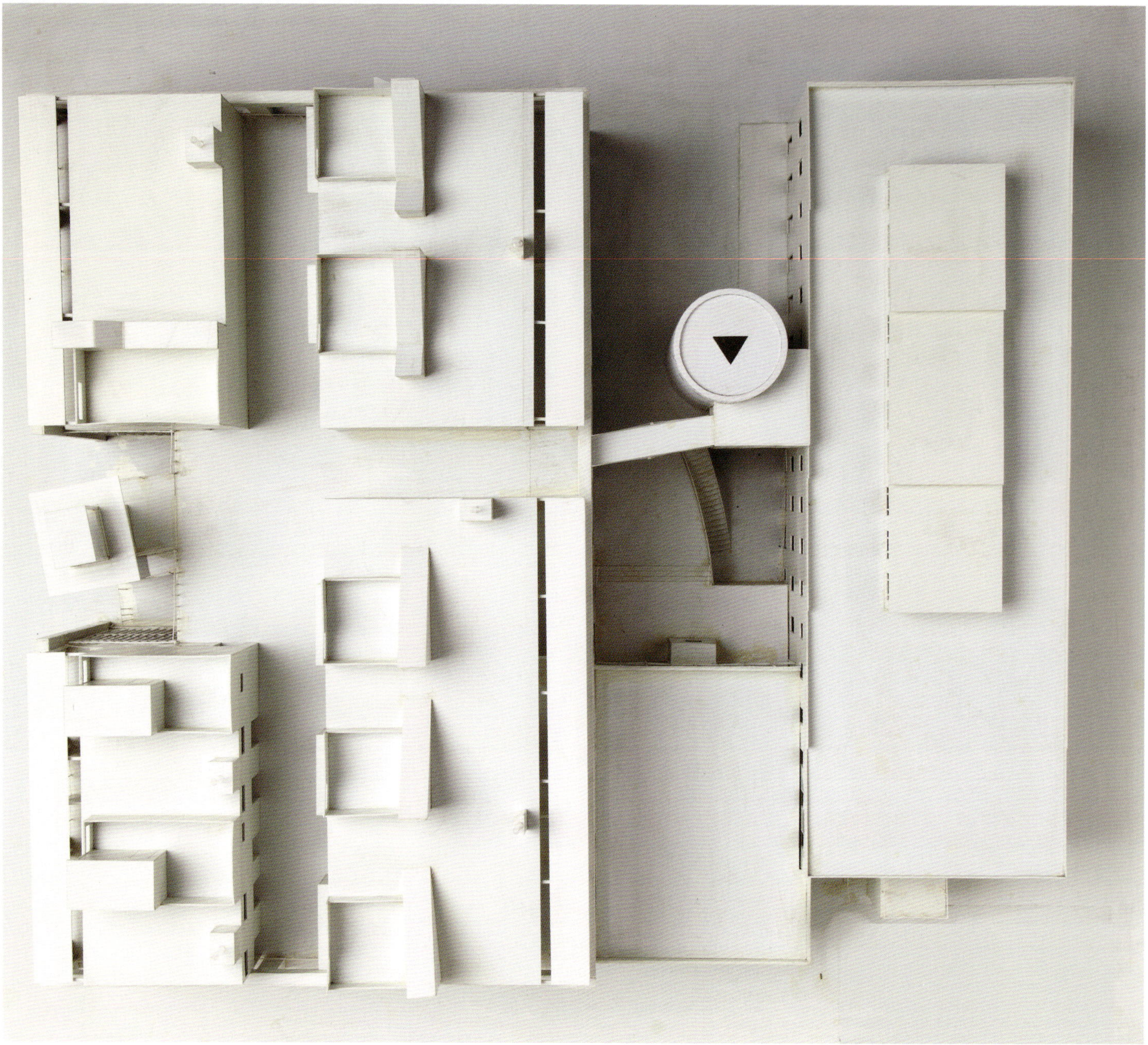

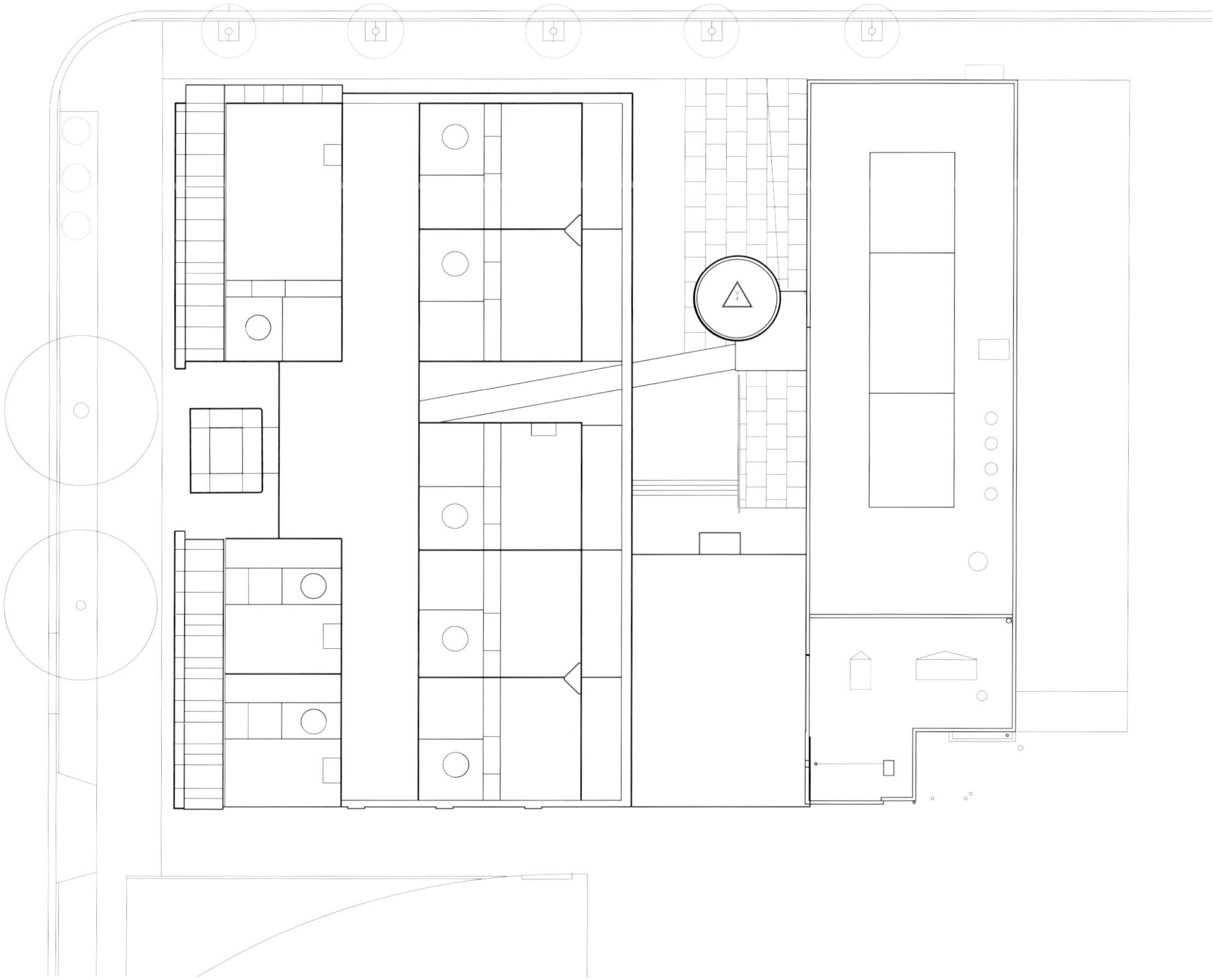

Site plan

32'

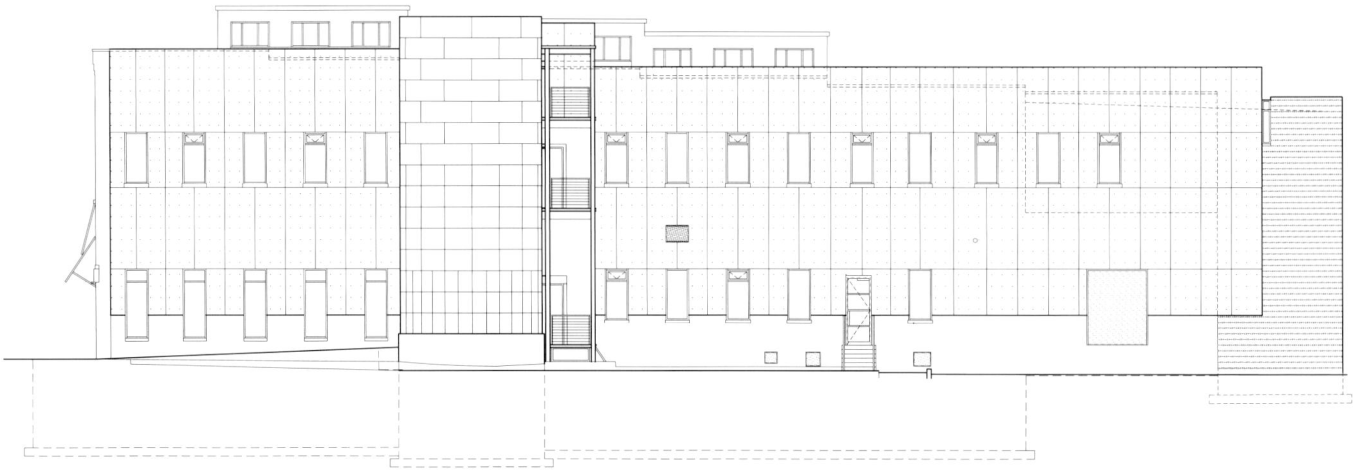

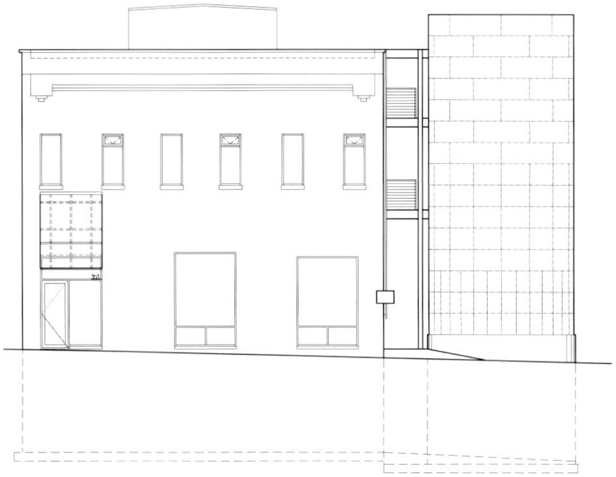

North elevation

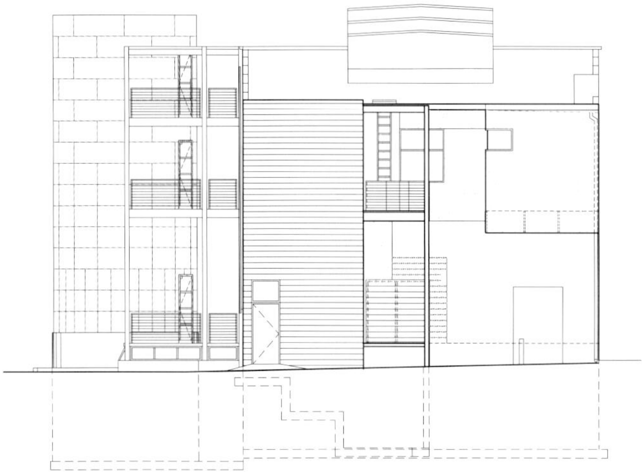

South elevation

32'

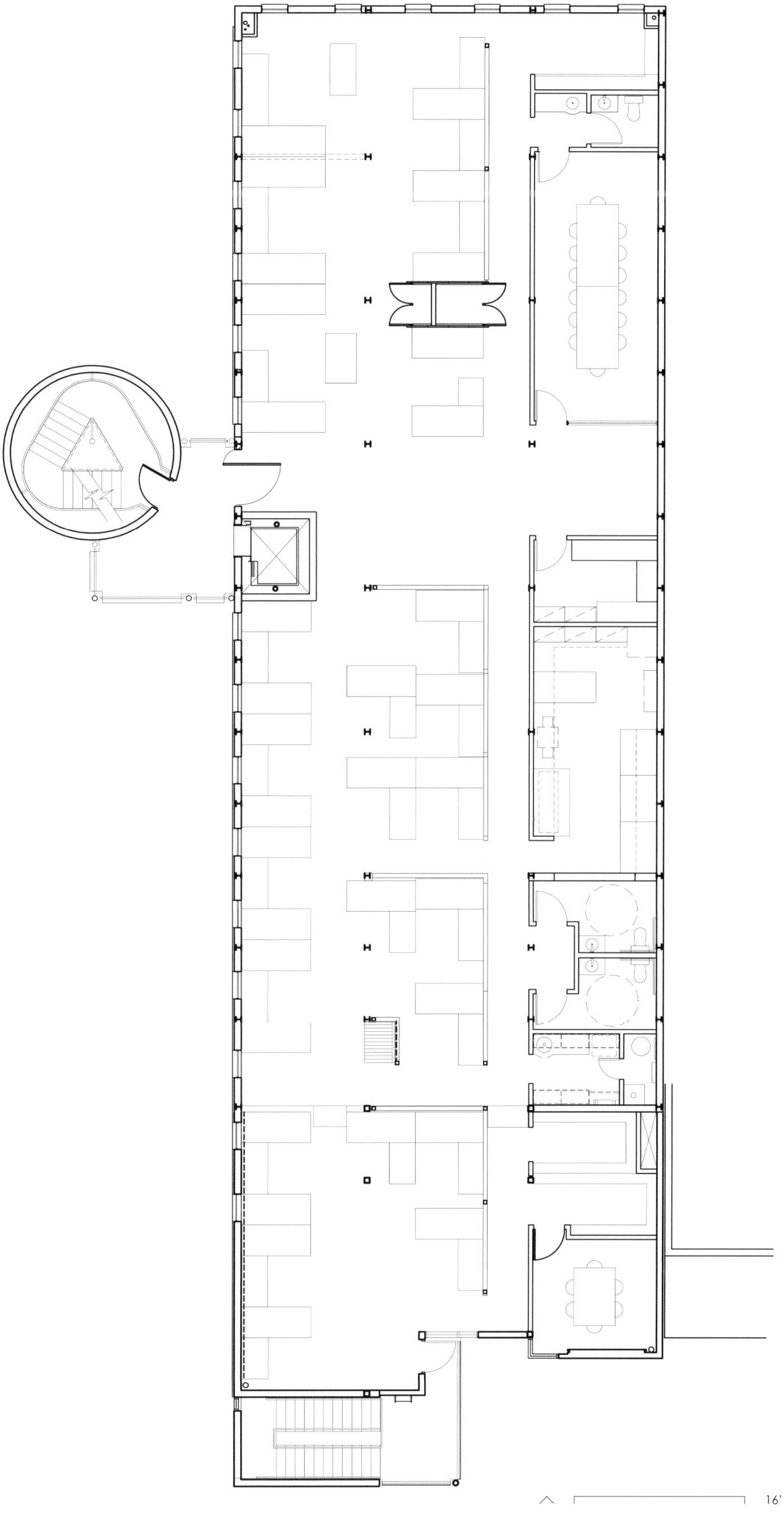

Second floor plan

ORD
NARY
L2

CAN SUBJECT MATTER

EXPLICIT

TANNER CHILDREN'S DANCE THEATER

Salt Lake City, Utah

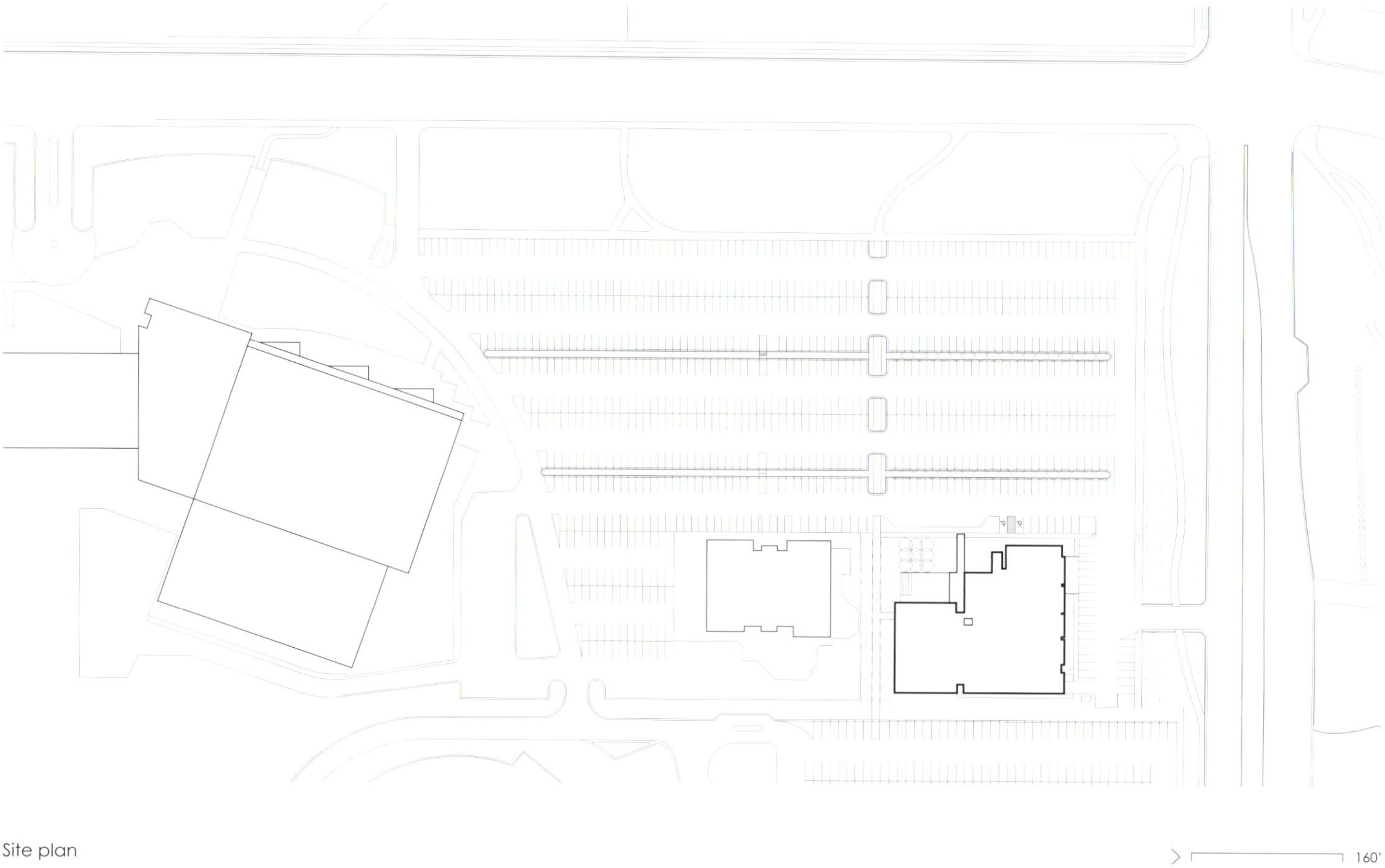

Site plan

The building confirms extensions of the body yet is subordinate to the activities held therein. This is a building whose presence is known and perceived upon arrival yet recedes as the children take possession of its internal spaces. Unlike a building for a professional ballet company, with its discrete and perfected spaces, this building invites dance in all its forms in corridors, stairs and dressing rooms. Chalk, ribbons and costumes are central props that are most immediate as objects to determine a narrative for path-finding and choreography. The building provides cast shadows and cropped views that focus attention. The passage of the sun across a wall and a graceful weathered surface induce the formation of childhood memory.

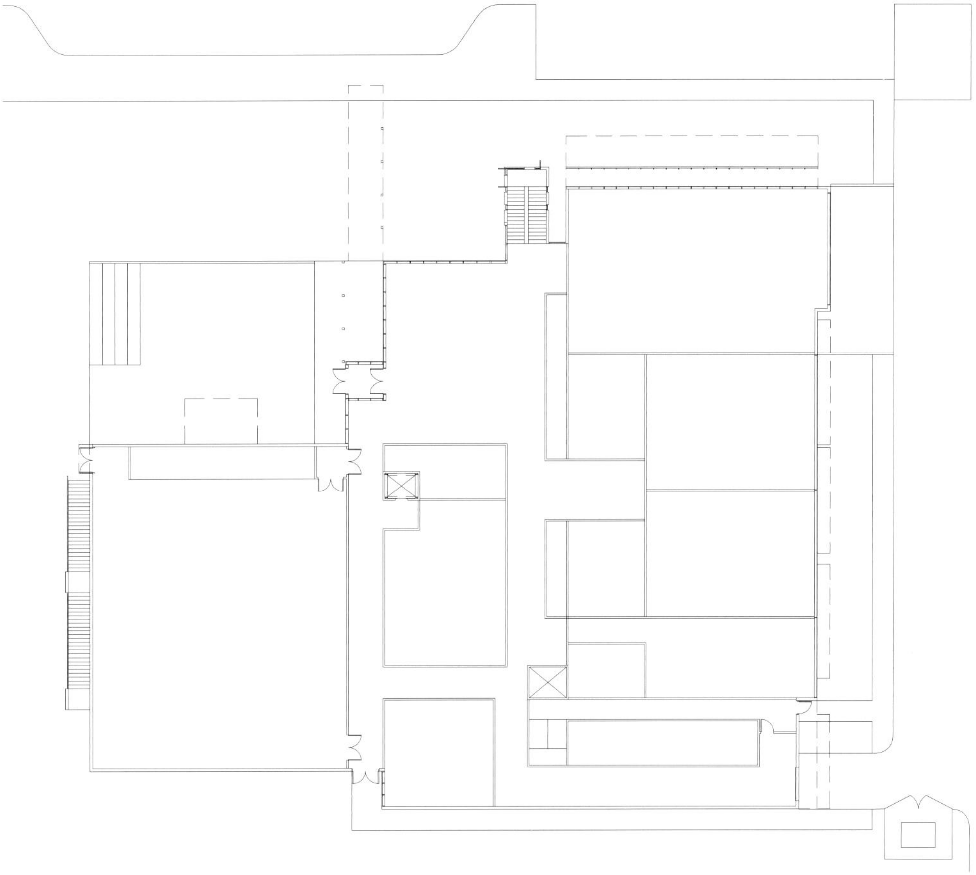

First floor plan

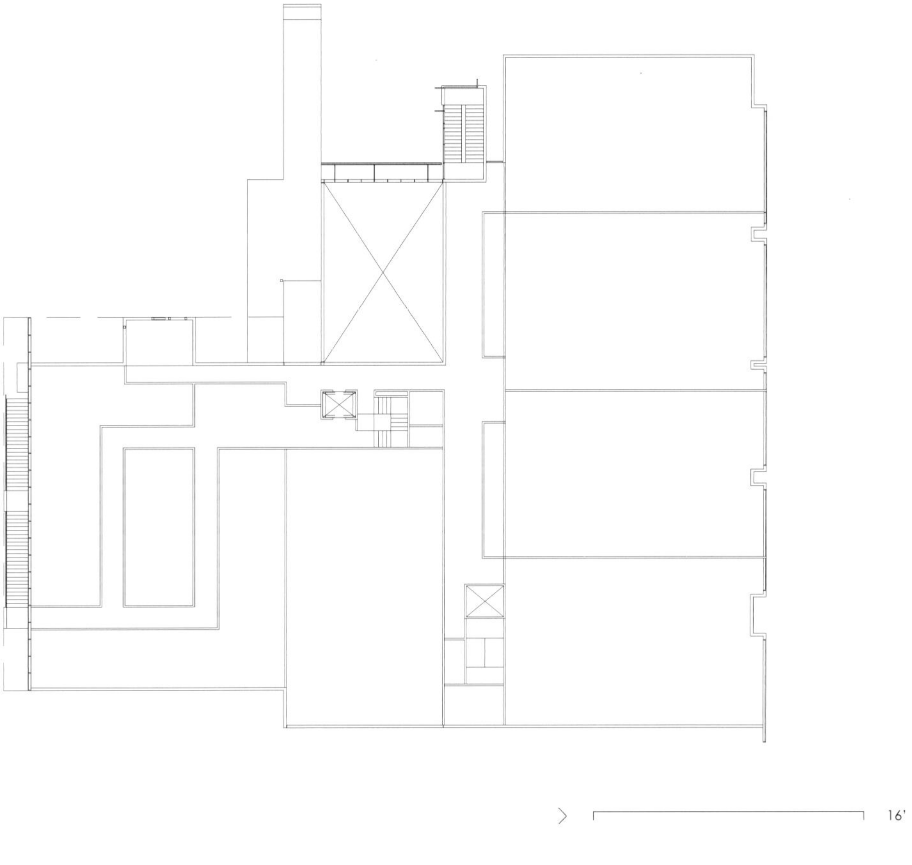

Second floor plan

BALLET WEST CONSERVATORY
Salt Lake City, Utah

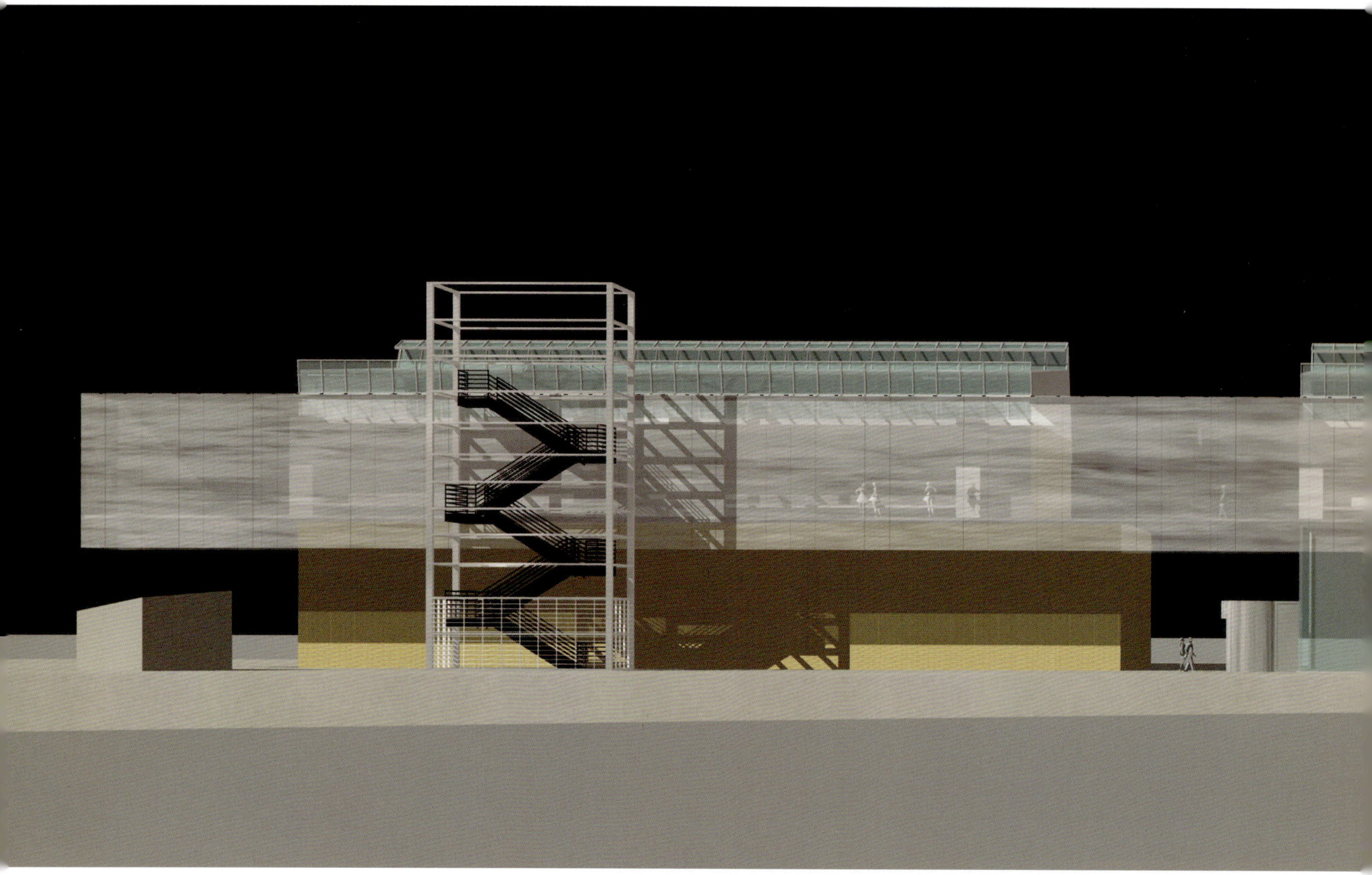

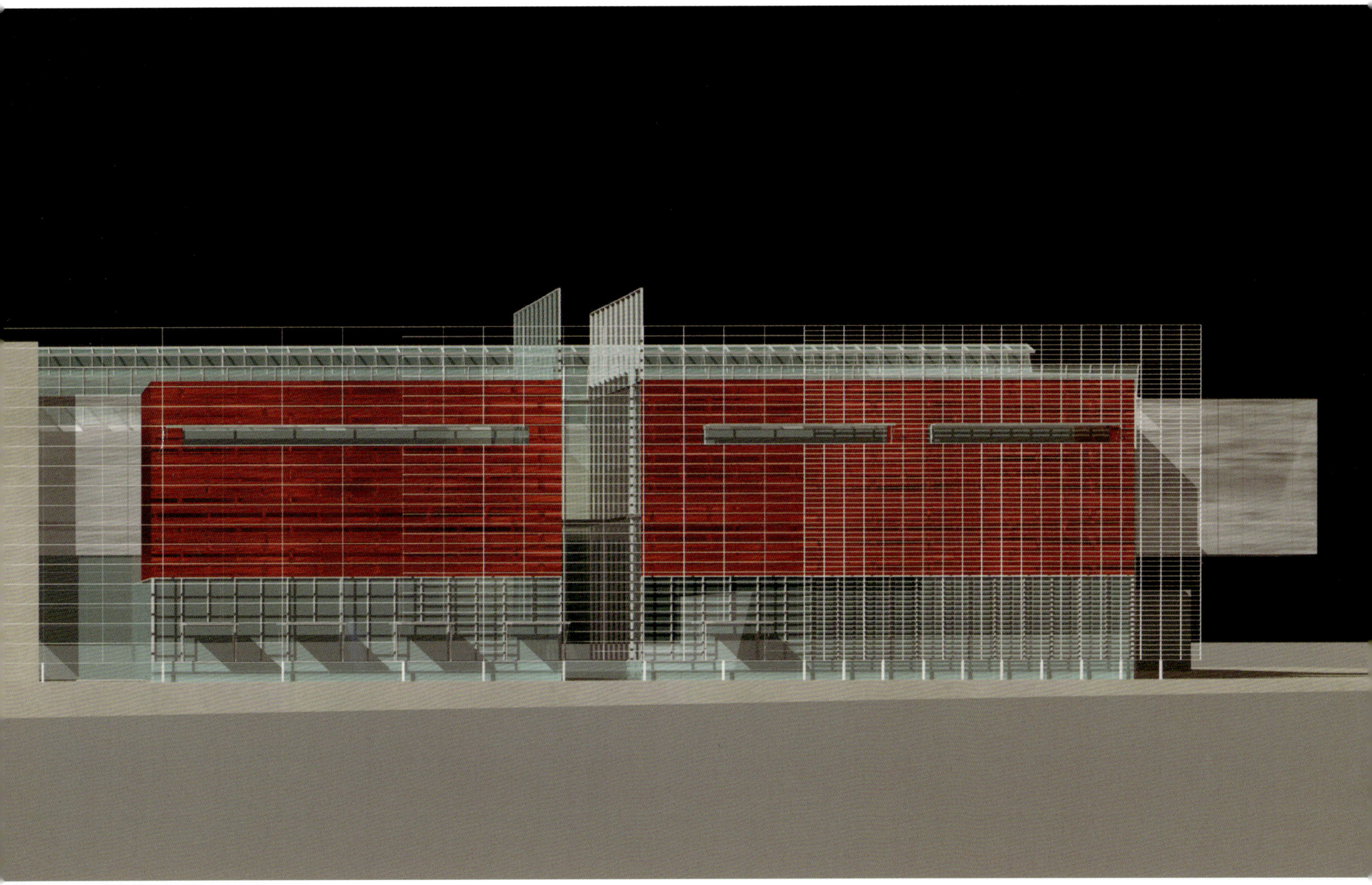

Design competitions are a challenge in they are executed with little credible engagement, which more often ends in disappointment, but the isolation of this exercise encourages new idea formation that can invariably emerge in subsequent work. A building for a dance company is the conjunction of opposites, that of the meditative nature of a disciplined and repetitive practice aspiring towards perfection and that of an informal gathering of community. The site provided a great opportunity to explore a similar juxtaposition of opposites from the public street on the south side to a nature park on the north. This northern orientation affords studios bathed in a cool blue light with pastoral views. The common areas could then be oriented to the yellow of south light, to which people normally gravitate in northern climates like Salt Lake. The design is composed of a series of veils or scrims that are layered through the building, ultimately revealing the park as viewed through the clear precision glass of the studios.

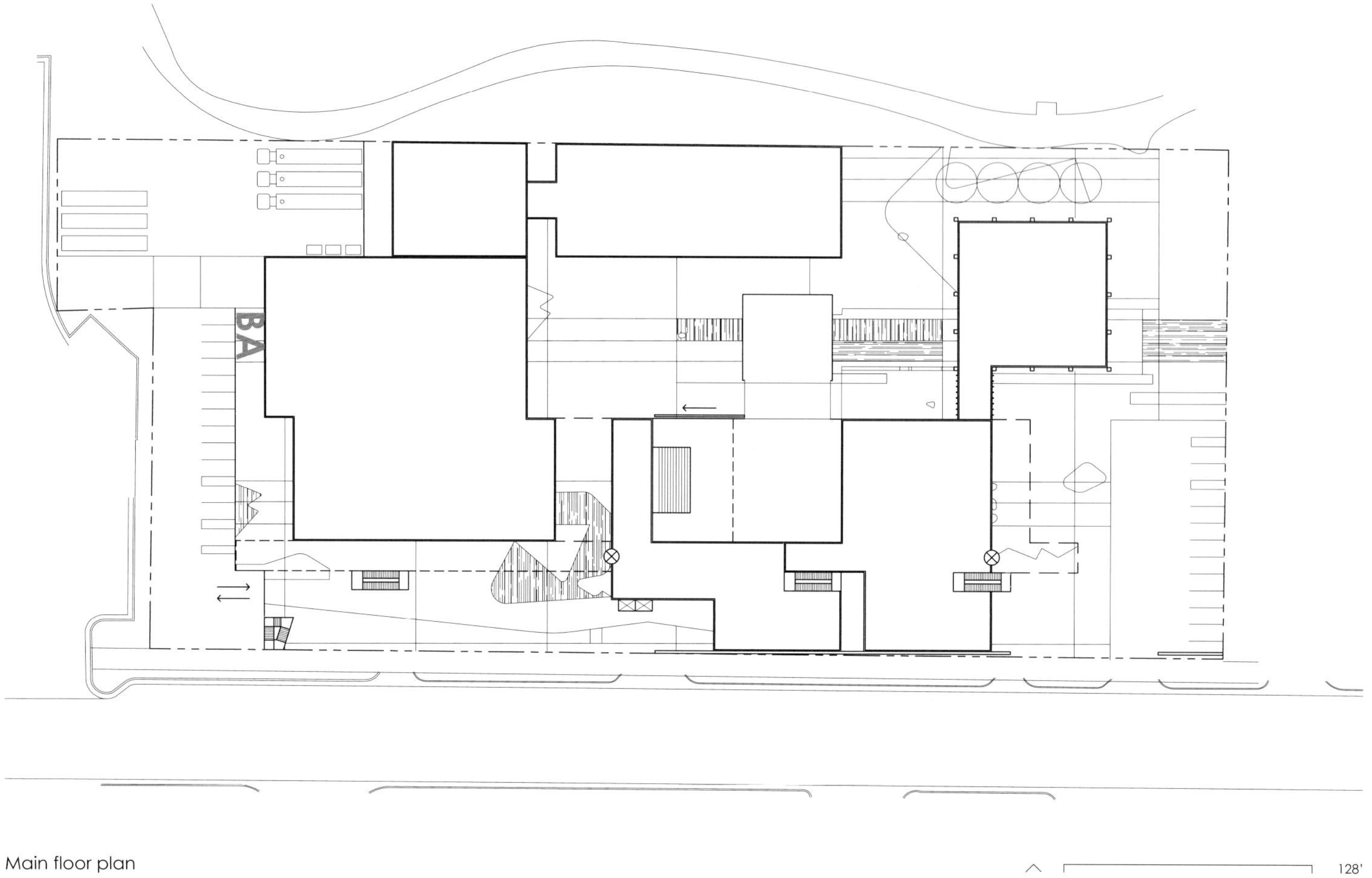

Main floor plan

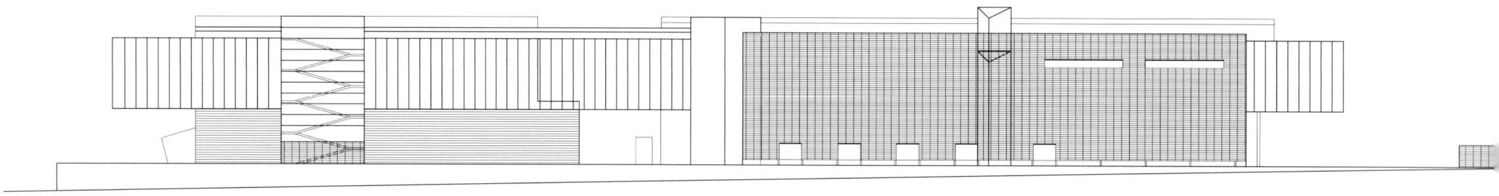

South elevation

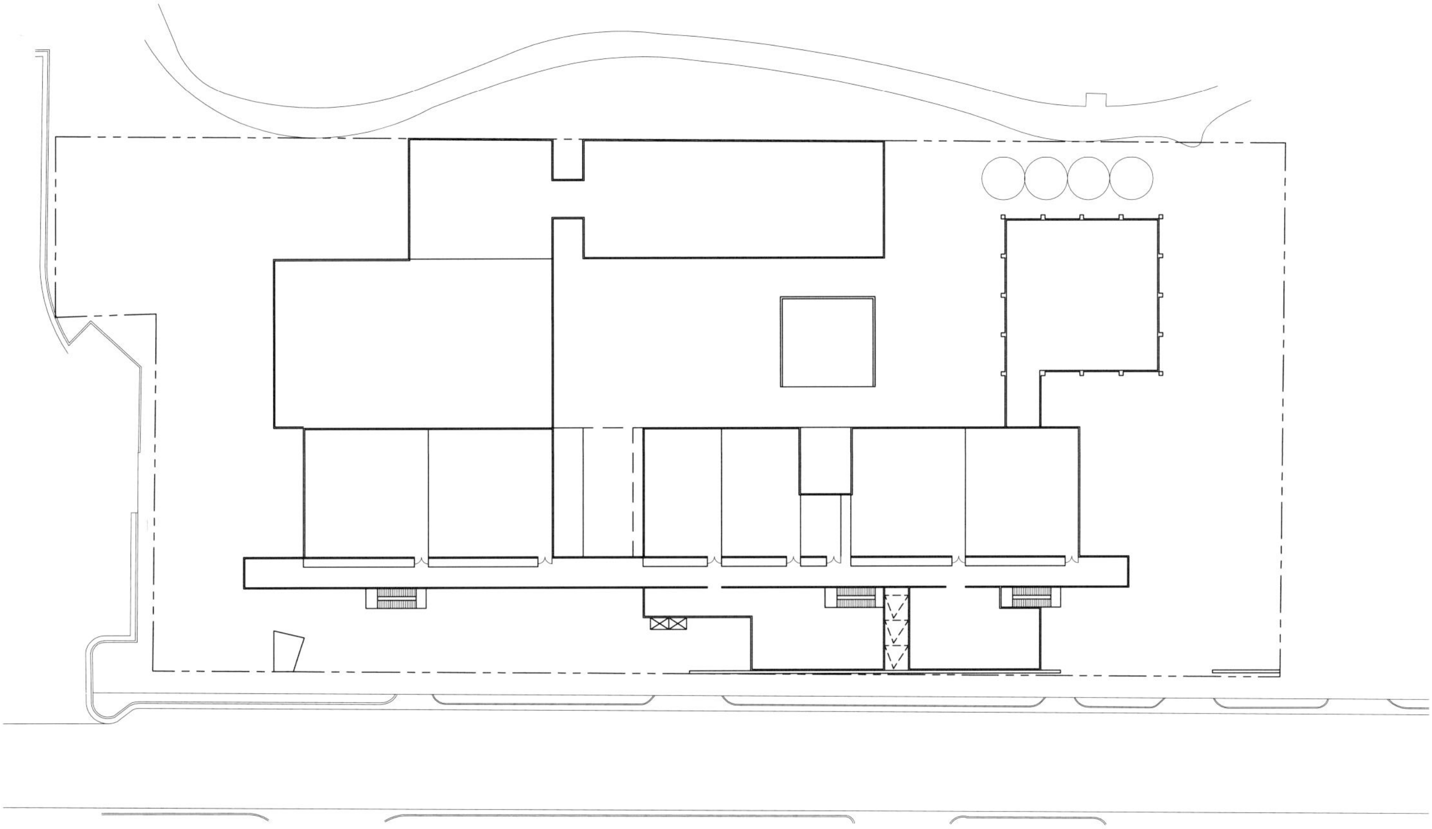

Second floor plan

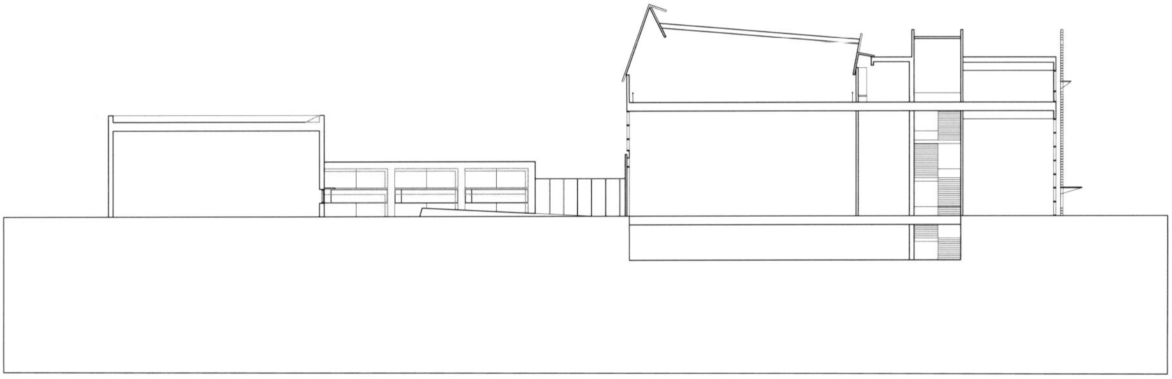

Cross section

ZION'S BANK DAYBREAK BRANCH

South Jordan, Utah

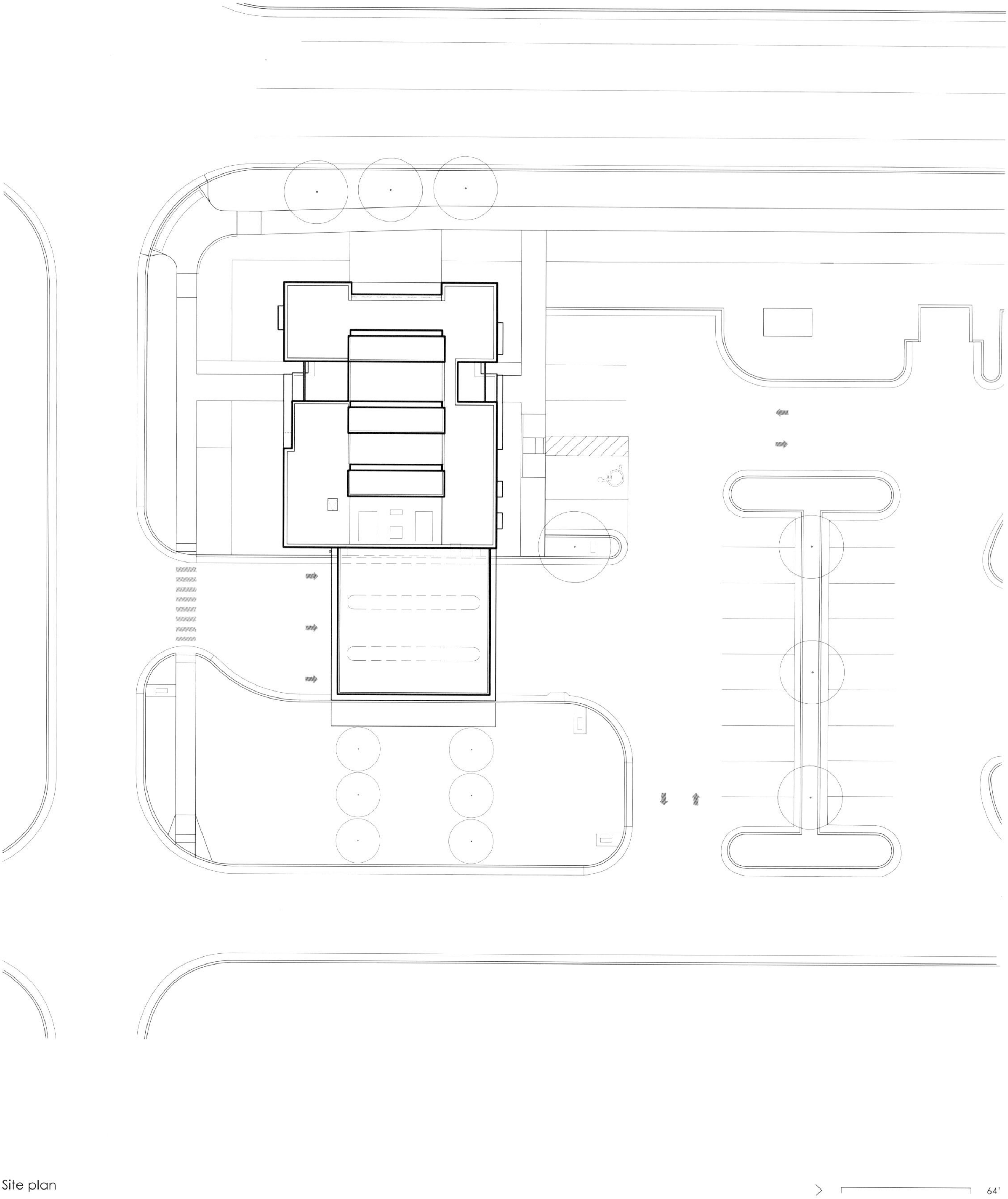

Site plan

The evolution of object buildings began with the Renaissance's simple measurement and recording of space, and later, with the Enlightenment, the commodification of time and space as vehicles for the ascendance of the middle class. The Zion's Bank building in Day Break, Utah is a celebration of the object building that draws meaning from the suburban condition. The materials reflect the amber of dusty conditions found in the newness of suburban sprawl and the crisp detailing of automobiles. This is a building that evinces precision, stability and the presence of an autonomous object.

Floor plan

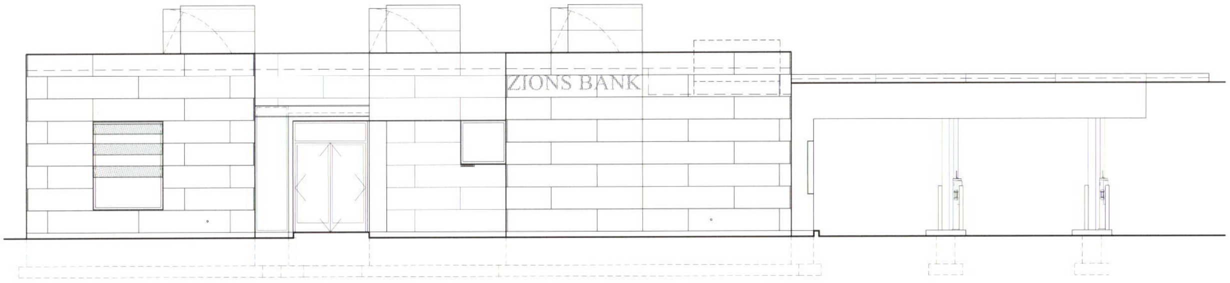

South elevation

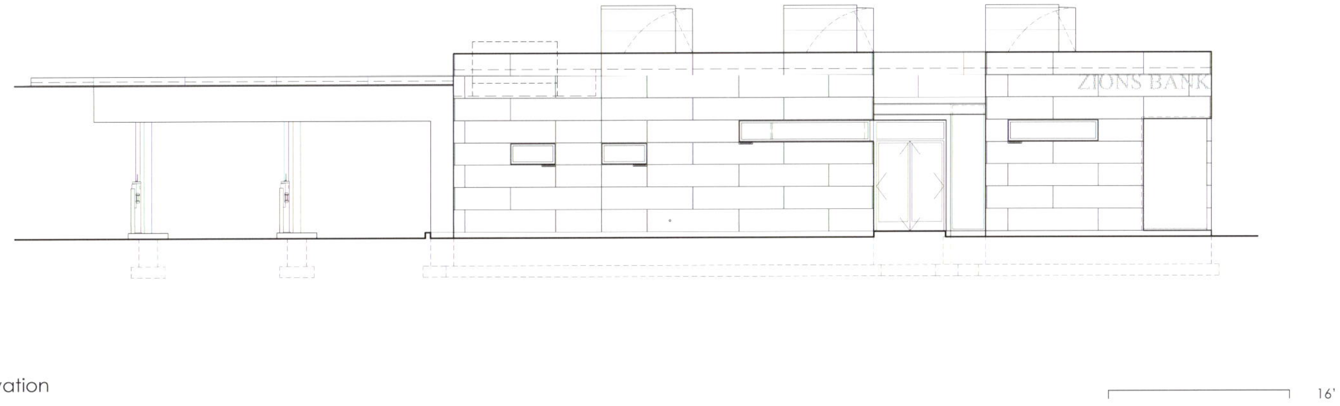

North elevation

HUMAN RIGHTS AND REMEMBRANCE MUSEUM

Salt Lake City, Utah

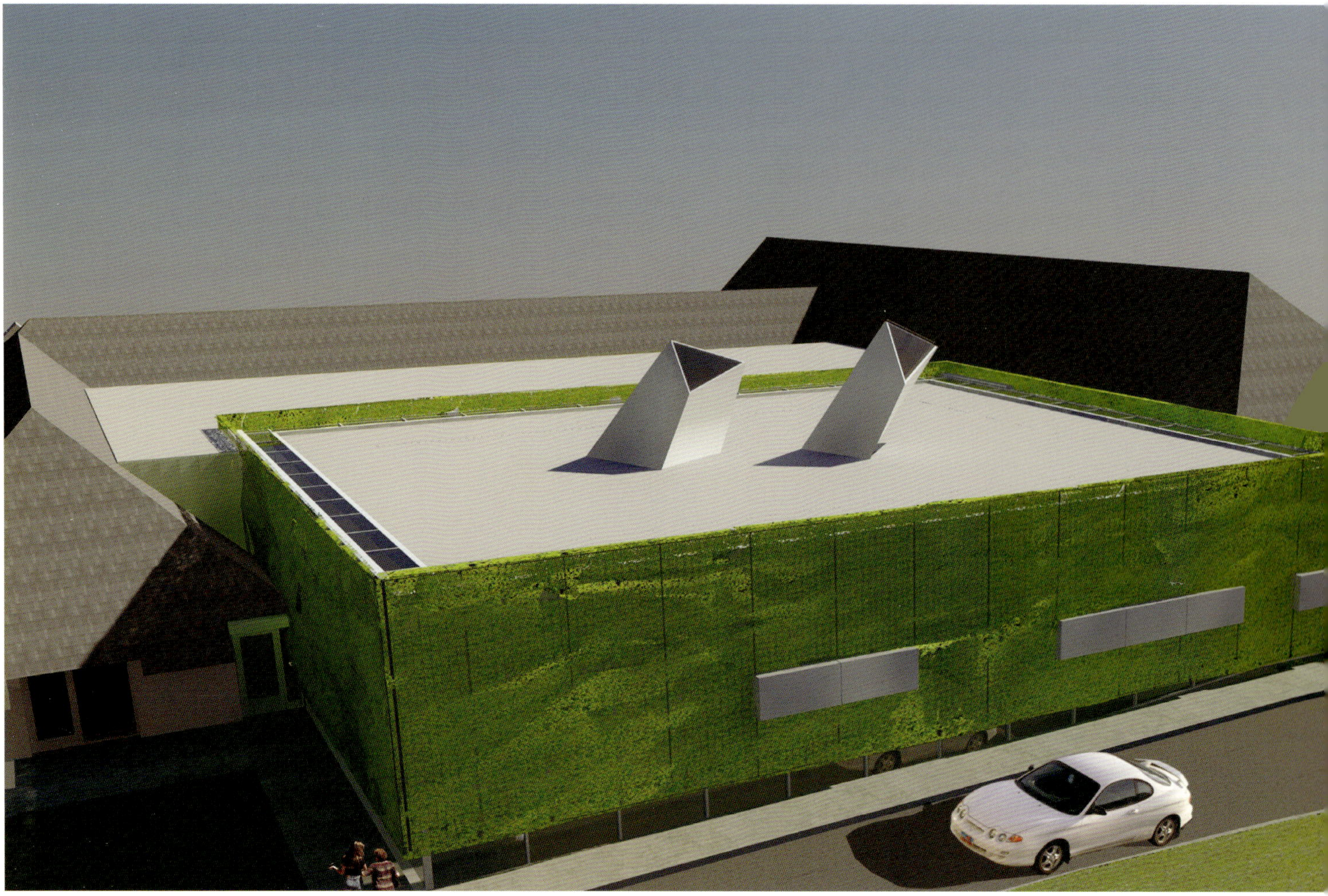

In the Wagner Jewish Community Center in Salt Lake is the Price Holocaust Memorial Garden design by Wendy Joseph. The community wanted to expand the mission of the garden to include an educational component that could extend the memorial message to include current issues in a provocative and engaging way. The design endeavored to reconcile the less-than-successful previous additions to the building into a both literal and figurative nexus for the institution. The existing garden is a contemplative and static display appropriate to a memorial. The new design aspires to a more active envelope that literally changes with the seasons yet invites a filtered light down through the layered ramp system to illuminate the memorial in a dramatic shaft of light reinforcing the archival quality of the piece.

PASSENGER
VEHICLES
ONLY
NO
TRUCKS
OR
BUSES

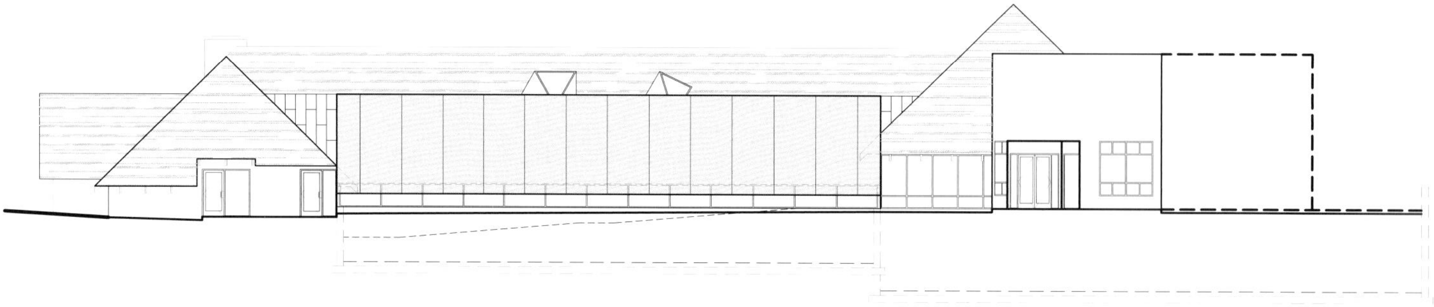

North elevation

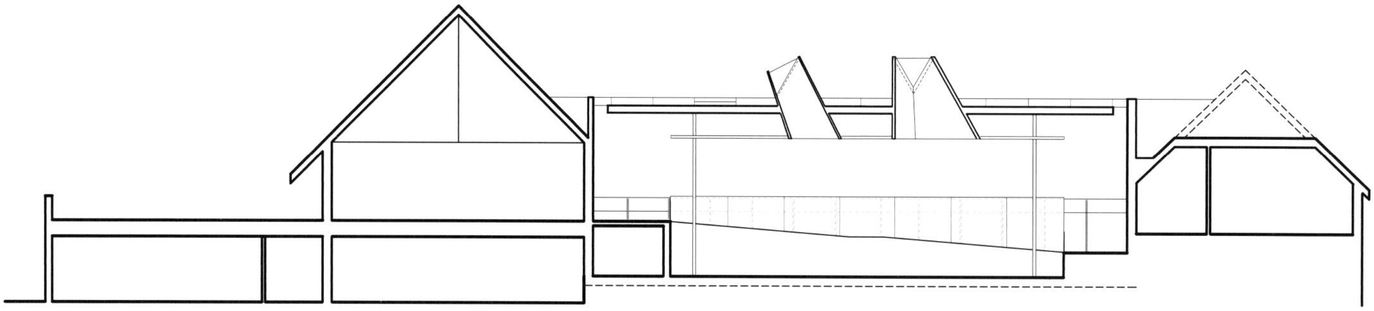

Long section

32'

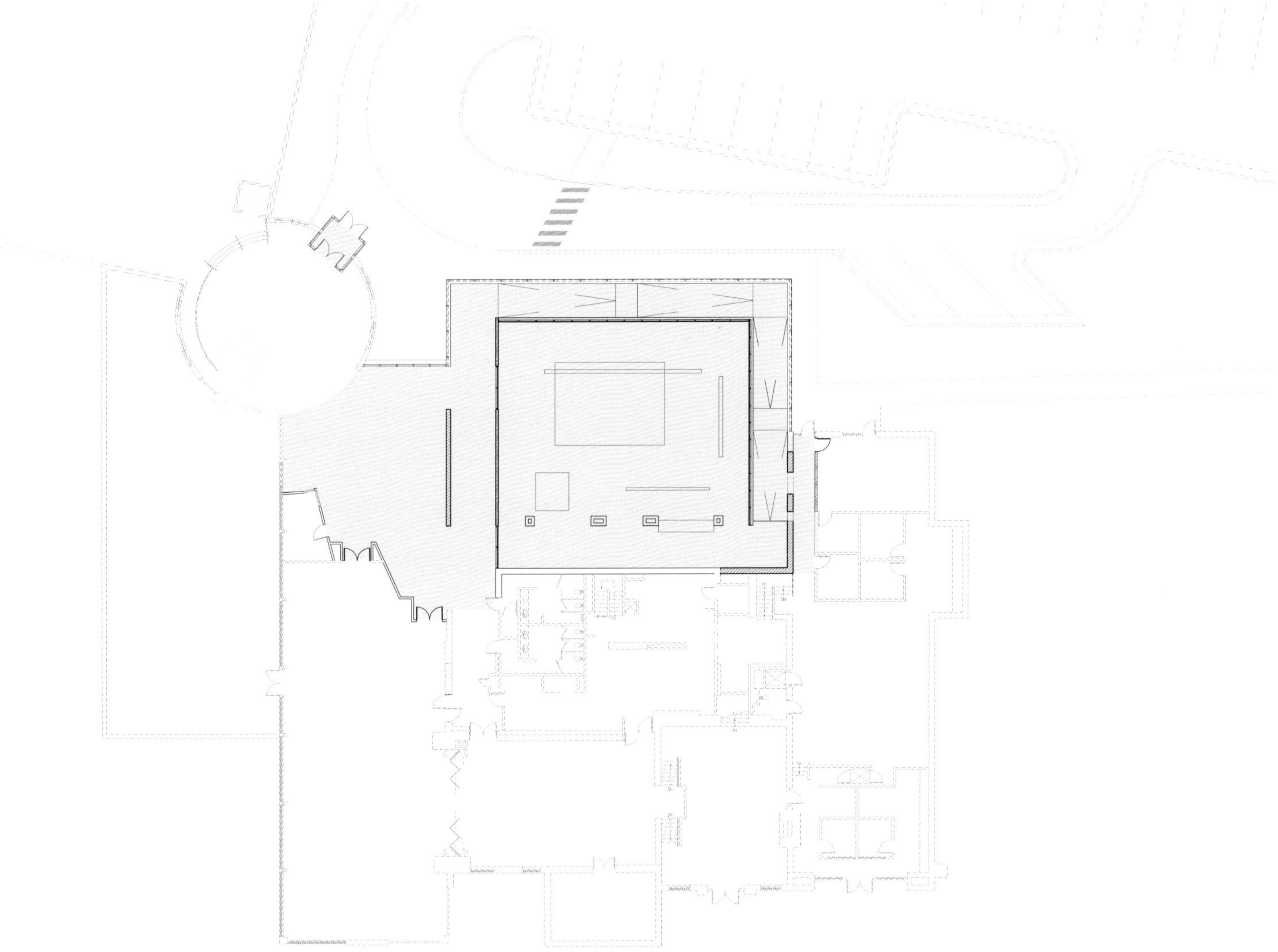

Second floor plan

MICHIGAN AVENUE RESIDENCE

Salt Lake City, Utah

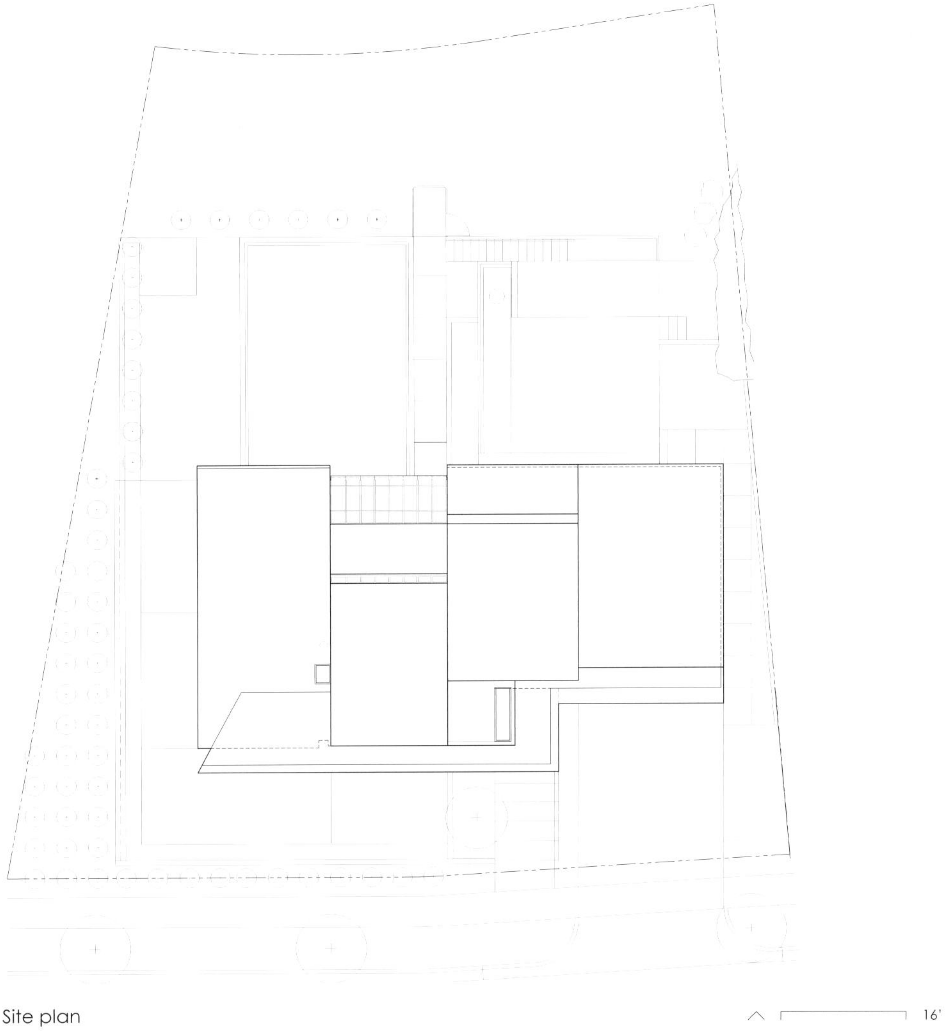

Site plan

The house is for a couple who wanted an understated residence in a respectful relationship to its neighbors, and that would not be part of the existing narrative but certainly in tune with its underlying rhythms, light and shadows. The design provides three conjoined pavilions identified by different roof forms. The two bookends provide utilitarian or service support to the exhibit and entertainment pavilion at the center. This living space mediates between the formal streetscape at the south and the expansive landscape revealed by the views to the north, including access to the deep gulley beyond.

Through these inner-city neighborhoods course the gulleys and waterways of the original drainage from the mountains in a sort of push and pull between the superimposed street grid and the memory of a non-compliant topography. The basement walls of the original house were kept and the new house was superimposed on the smaller footprint of the original. The house aspires to be part of the site by reflecting the deep recesses of the adjoining bungalows on the street side with extended eaves that provide a passive solar interior. The brick veneer reflects the modular building material of the neighborhood transforms from load bearing on the uphill side to a dematerialized glass brick at the cantilever bedroom wing. Although its origins trascend its identiy, the house aspires to be very much its own entity.

1395

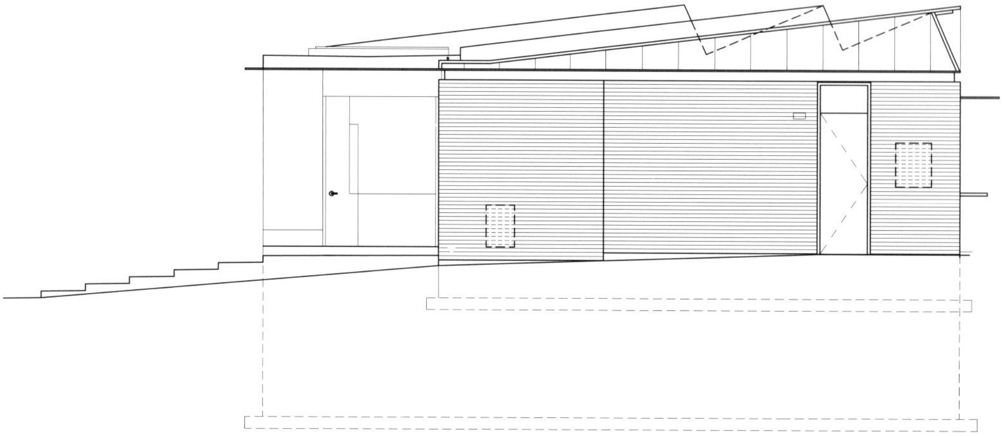

East elevation

West elevation

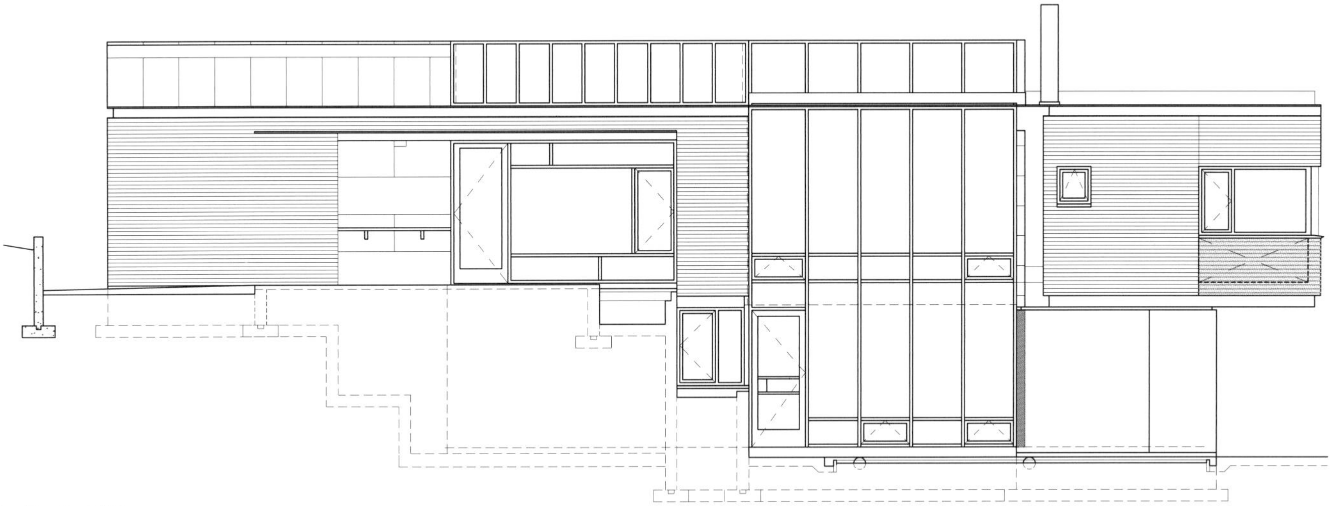

North elevation

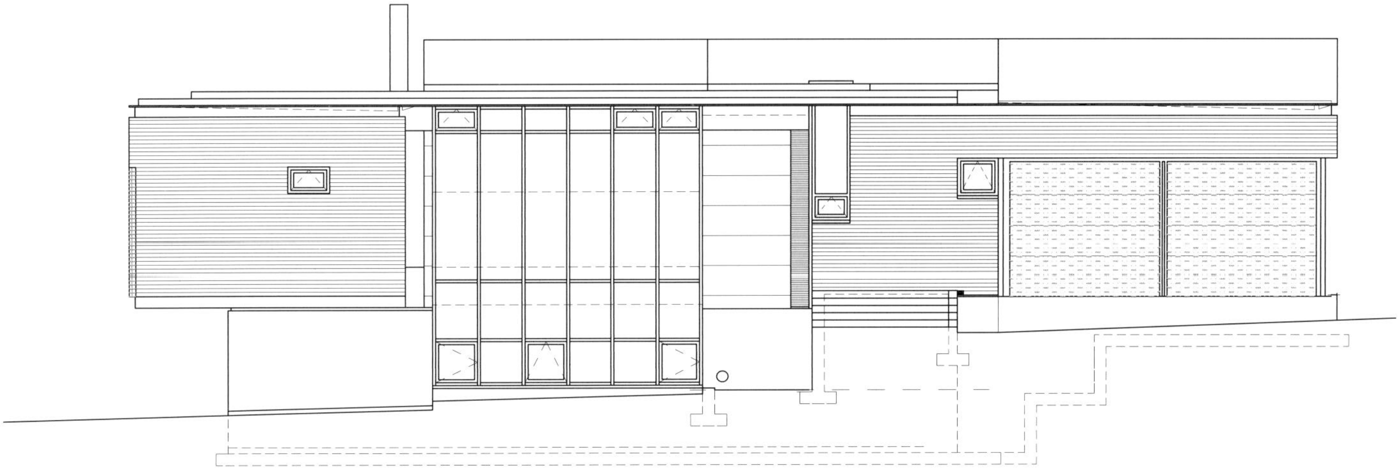

South elevation

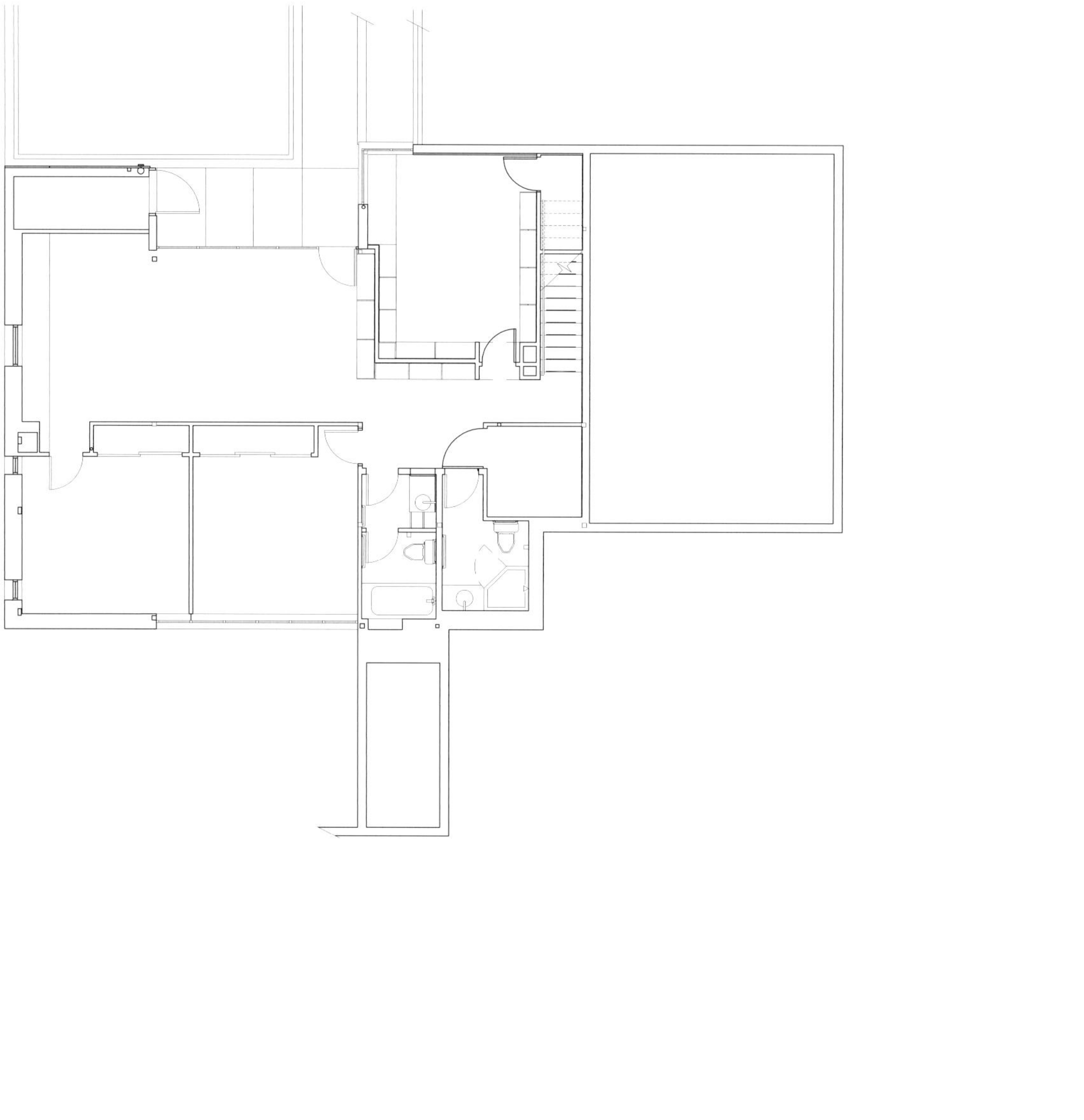

Lower floor plan

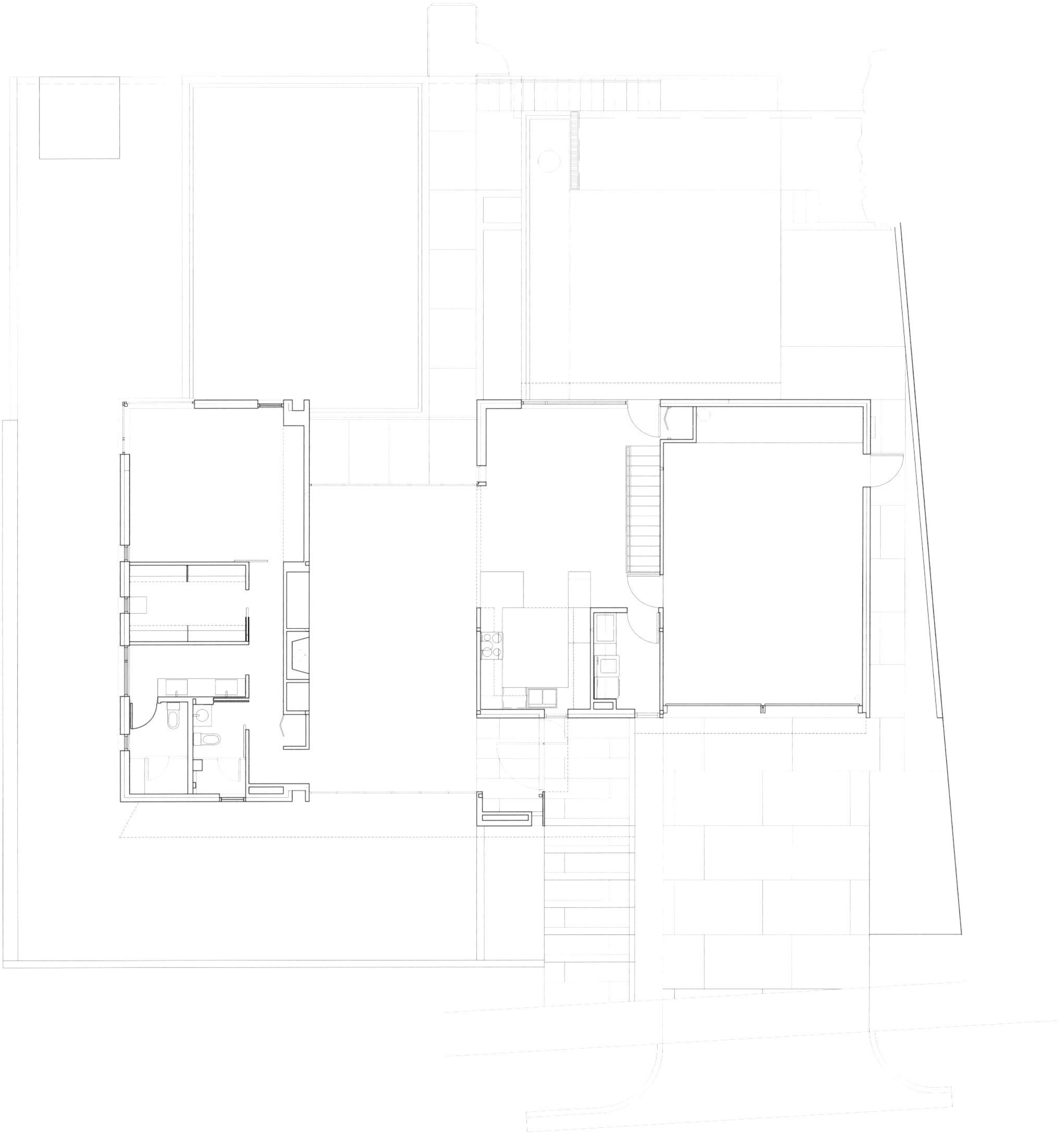

Main floor plan

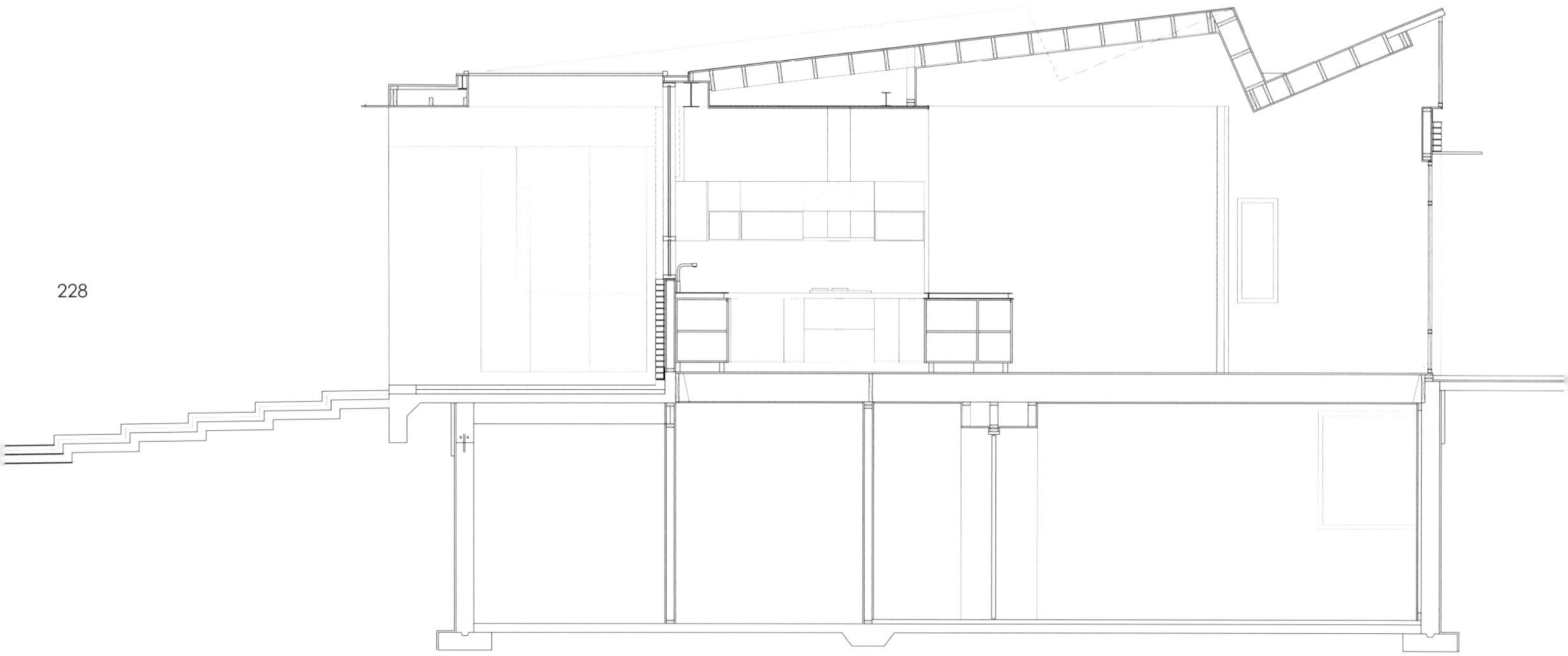

Cross section

This world that I had created like a man digging a well with a needle would then seem truer than all else

Orhan Pamuk, *Other Colors: Essay and a Story.*

APPENDIX

FIRM PROFILE

 Prescott Muir formed the architecture practice in 1976 with offices in Los Angeles and Salt Lake City. He graduated from the University of Southern California at the tail end of the Case Study House era and later at Columbia University's GSAPP. The firm has received numerous design awards and recognition in the national architectural press. In 2008, Muir was elevated in the design category to the college of Fellows of the American Institute of Architects. He has lectured extensively and in 2009 was appointed Professor in Architecture and Director of the School of Architecture at the University of Utah. Muir's Partners in the firm, Lisa Arnett, Jack Robertson, and Jay Lems have over the last 20 years contributed much to the success of the work.

ACKNOWLEDGEMENTS

CURRENT STAFF

PRESCOTT MUIR
LISA ARNETT PARTNER
JACK ROBERTSON PARTNER
JAY LEMS PARTNER
COREY CRACROFT
KRYSTA DIMICK
THEO HASKINS
TINA HEALY
JARED LARSON
THOMAS MORAHAN
BRIAN STARKEY
KRISTEN VOROS

PAST STAFF

LYNN ATWOOD
CHRIS BACHOROWSKI
MERATE BARAKAT
KATHY BLACK
SHARON BLAKE
PAULA CARL
DEBRA CARUSO
RICHARD CHONG
CHRIS CLARK
TAMI CLEVELAND
CHRIS CORDREY
JONATHAN DAZLEY
RAND ERDLY
PIERRE FAGERLUND
DAVID FITZSIMMONS
BERNARDO FLORES-SAHAGUN
DANIEL FOSTE
SARAH FOSTER
GREG FREEMAN
KAREN FUUKENGER
GARY GOWERS
AARON HANSEN
LIBBY HASLAM
SHARON HAURI
TROY HAYNES
KIRA LABRUM
JANET LANG
LINDSEY LEITHEAD
BRUCE LINDSEY
BEE LOESSE
BLAKE LUTHOR
JOHN MAGNUS-ABLE
SOPHIE MASSE
GREG MAYNES
PAT MCLAUGHLAN
MENDOZA MARIO
CALEB MENGE
NAIMA NAWABI
ELIZABETH NEBECKER
CHRIS NELSON
JEFF NEWMAN
DAN OGURA
CLAIRE OLSEN
ROB ORTEN
LARRY ORTON
CONNIE PAVLICAS
DEREK PAYNE
BETTY PERNG
DOUG PRUITT
PATRICIA PRYNE
JOY PUGSLEY
DAVE PUGSLEY
JONATHAN RAMAS
JACK RENNER
BRIAN RUSSELL
BONNIE SCOTT
MEAGAN SMUIN
MARK STONEHAWKER
GEORGE STROMQUIST
HALEY TESSIER
ELPITHA TSOUTSOUNAKIS
BOYD UEHLIG
TOM VAUGHN
GREG WALKER
MICHAEL WESCOATT
LAURA WHIPPLE
RAY WHITCHURCH
ROB WHITE
ROBERT WHITE
JENNIFER WILLIAMS
DWIGHT YEE
TONY YOUNGBLOOD

BOOK CREDITS

238 PHOTOGRAPHY
Scott Peterson, Photographer
Scot Zimmerman, Photographer
Jan Andrews, Photographer, Cinematographer
Lisa Arnett

ILLUSTRATIONS
Thomas Morahan
Troy Haynes

PROJECT PARTICIPATION
Aden Ross, Writer
Ric Collier, Artist

ORO *editions*
Gordon Goff, Publisher
Pablo Mandel, Book Design
Usana Shadday, Production Manager

ENDORSEMENTS

RODOLFO MACHADO
Professor of Architecture & Urban Design, Co-Chair Urban Planning & Design Department of Graduate School of Design, Harvard University Graduate School of Design, Boston, Massachusetts

In the cultural landscape of Utah, Prescott Muir is a unique figure: a very good architect whose interest in the regional context is always as contemporary as it is un-sentimental, and a teacher under whose guidance the School of Architecture will be updated and enriched by new developments while remaining solidly grounded on architectural discipline.

BRUCE LINDSEY, AIA
Dean E. Desmond Lee Professor of Architecture & Urban Planning, Washington University St. Louis, Missouri

I have known Mr. Muir over 25 years. For 30 years his work has been characterized by formal innovation, programmatic sophistication and material exploration, all the while gaining national recognition. Spanning master planning, large-scale institutional projects, residential and exhibition design, Muir and his office has consistently produced work that is generated by its context and at the same time regenerates a new and evolving context, whether at the scale of a house or a city.

ORO *editions*
Publishers of Architecture, Art and Design
Gordon Goff—Publisher
www.oroeditions.com
info@oroeditions.com

IT BY BIT

ISBN: 978-1-9359350-5-6

Writers:
Prescott Muir
Juhani Uolevi Pallasmaa
Dan Hoffman

Book Design:
Pablo Mandel / CircularStudio

Photography:
Scott Peterson, Photographer
Scot Zimmerman, Photographer
Jan Andrews, Photographer, Cinematographer
Lisa Arnett

Illustrations:
Thomas Morahan
Troy Haynes

Project Participation:
Aden Ross, Writer
Ric Collier, Artist

Produced by ORO *editions*
Production Manager: Usana Shadday
Production Assistance: Gabriel Ely
Project Coordinator: Christy LaFaver
Color Separation and Printing: ORO *group* Ltd
Text printed using offset sheetfed printing process in 4 color
on 157gsm premium matt coated artpaper.
Printed in China.

Library of Congress Cataloging-in-Publication Data Available.

ORO *editions* has made every effort to minimize the overall carbon footprint of this project. As part of this goal, ORO *editions*, in association with Global ReLeaf, has arranged to plant two trees for each and every tree used in the manufacturing of the paper produced for this book. Global ReLeaf is an international campaign run by American Forests, the nation's oldest nonprofit conservation organization. Global ReLeaf is American Forests' education and action program that helps individuals, organizations, agencies, and corporations improve the local and global environment by planting and caring for trees.